THE ENGLISH KITCHEN

Frontispiece. 'A Modern Ball Buffet', from Theodore Francis Garrett, ed., The Encylopaedia of Practical Cookery *(c. 1895).*

THE
ENGLISH KITCHEN

HISTORICAL ESSAYS

LEEDS SYMPOSIUM ON FOOD HISTORY
'FOOD AND SOCIETY' SERIES

edited by

EILEEN WHITE

PROSPECT BOOKS

2007

First published in 2007 by Prospect Books, Allaleigh House, Blackawton, Totnes, Devon TQ9 7DL.

Based on papers from the Eighteenth Leeds Symposium on Food History, March 2003, 'The Changing Face of Food'. This is the thirteenth volume in the series 'Food and Society'.

BRITISH LIBRARY CATALOGUING IN PUBLICATION DATA:
A catalogue entry for this book is available from the British Library.

ISBN 978-1-903018-50-7

Typeset by Tom Jaine.
Printed and bound by the Cromwell Press, Trowbridge, Wiltshire.

CONTENTS

ACKNOWLEDGEMENTS

To the staff, past and present, of Special Collections in the Brotherton Library, University of Leeds, are due thanks for their friendly service over many years of research by the contributors to this volume. Unless otherwise stated in the captions, all illustrations are taken from Eliza Acton, *Modern Cookery, for Private Families* (1856 edition) and Theodore Francis Garrett, ed., *The Encyclopaedia of Modern Cookery* (c. 1895). The second title was used by kind permission of Mr C. Sheppard, the Special Collections Librarian.

FOREWORD

'Food and Society' Series
Publication of papers from the Leeds Symposium on Food History

The first six volumes were published by Edinburgh University Press and are now out of print; the following three by Sutton Publishing (two of them in association with The National Trust); the volumes from no. 10 have been published by Prospect Books. The titles, with the series numbers, are:

1. *'Banquetting Stuffe': the Fare and Social Background of the Tudor and Stuart Banquet*, ed. C.A. Wilson (1986 Symposium), 1991.

2. *The Appetite and the Eye: Visual Aspects of Food and its Presentation within their Historic Context*, ed. C.A. Wilson (1987 Symposium), 1991.

3. *Traditional Food East and West of the Pennines*, ed. C.A. Wilson (1988 Symposium), 1991.

4. *Waste Not, Want Not: Food Preservation in Britain from Early Times to the Present Day*, ed. C.A. Wilson (1989 Symposium), 1991.

5. *Liquid Nourishment: Potable Foods and Stimulating Drinks*, ed. C.A. Wilson (1990 Symposium), 1993.

6. *Food for the Community: Special Diets for Special Groups*, ed. C.A. Wilson (1991 Symposium), 1993.

7. *Luncheon, Nuncheon and Other Meals*, ed. C.A. Wilson (1992 Symposium), 1994. Now republished in paperback as *Eating with the Victorians* (Sutton, 2004).

8. *The Country House Kitchen, 1650–1900: Skills and Equipment for Food Provisioning*, ed. P.A. Sambrook and P. Brears (double volume for 1993 and 1994 Symposia), 1996.

9. *The Country House Kitchen Garden, 1600–1950: How Produce was Grown and How it was Used*, ed. C.A. Wilson (1995 Symposium), 1998.

10. *Feeding a City: York*, ed. E. White (double volume for 1997 and 1998 Symposia), 2000.

11. *Food and the Rites of Passage*, ed. L. Mason (1999 Symposium), 2002.

12. *The English Cookery Book*, ed. E. White (2001 Symposium), 2004.

NOTES ON CONTRIBUTORS

TOM JAINE is publisher of Prospect Books.

FIONA LUCRAFT is an independent scholar of English food history. Among her articles, she has contributed a study of Hannah Glasse's plagiarisms to *Petits Propos Culinaires*.

GILLY LEHMANN is Professor of English at the University of Franche-Comté at Besançon and author of *The British Housewife: Cookery Books, Cooking and Society in Eighteenth-Century Britain*.

LAURA MASON is a regular contributor to the Leeds Food Symposium. She has written a history of sweets, *Sugar Plums and Sherbet*, is co-author of *The Taste of Britain*, and author of the National Trust's book of English recipes.

ANN RYCRAFT is a teaching fellow in the Centre for Medieval Studies at the University of York, where she teaches palaeography and manuscript studies. She convenes a group working on York cookery manuscripts and food documents from the fifteenth to the nineteenth centuries.

EILEEN WHITE began researching in the cookery collection at the Brotherton Library after becoming interested in recreating old recipes for period suppers at Bolling Hall Museum in Bradford. She has contributed several papers to the 'Food and Society' series, and compiled the volume *Soup* for the Prospect series on the English kitchen.

C. ANNE WILSON is the overall editor for the 'Food and Society' series. Her most recent book, *Water of Life*, a study of the history of wine-distilling and spirits, is published by Prospect Books.

PREFACE

Eileen White

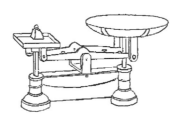

The papers collected here were originally presented to the eighteenth Leeds Symposium on Food History as 'The Changing Face of Food'. The inspiration for the day came from Prospect Books' series under the general heading 'The English Kitchen', and that title has been given to this publication. 'English' in this case means the language in which the recipes are written rather than marking national boundaries.

Individual chapters reflect the enthusiasm of the contributors and do not cover the full range of food in Britain. Readers may be inspired to take their own item of food and track its progress through the ages. A single dish can reflect the changing taste of a nation, from the use of a profusion of spices and a mixture of sweet and savoury, to a deliberate limitation of flavours and division of dishes into specific courses. As literacy grew, and printed books became easily affordable, the recipes took in the simpler meals of all classes of society. They also reveal the gradual incorporation of ready-made flavours and thickeners, and the industrial provision of food that leaves little for the cook to do.

The contributors have made use of dictionary definitions in beginning their examination of a particular dish, but these definitions are framed by lexicographers rather than cooks. The next step is to consult the recipe books themselves, and favourites have emerged in the following chapters.

Many are available in modern transcriptions, editions or facsimiles, starting with medieval manuscripts care of the Early English Text Society and taking in the writings of Thomas Dawson, John Murrell, Robert May, Hannah Glasse, Martha Bradley and Eliza Acton. More books popular with contributors, available in collections such as those in the Brotherton Library of Leeds University, include Gervase Markham and Hannah Wolley. Mrs Beeton's original publication of 1861 is available in facsimile, and Mrs A.B. Marshall is becoming better known through the work of her present-day admirers. Publications of personal manuscripts, such as those of Elinor Fettiplace, Rebecca Price and John Evelyn, help to give a more domestic view of what was prepared in the English kitchen. Samuel Pepys and Grisell Baillie offer examples of meals actually eaten. Unpublished cookery manuscripts in private collections or public record offices will provide further examples of different dishes evolving over several generations. It is hoped that the following chapters will prompt others to track a favourite recipe as it evolved to suit tastes, availability of ingredients and technical advances in kitchen equipment.

The introduction by Tom Jaine poses the question lying behind the other chapters: is there something that can be defined as English cookery? The example he gives of produce available in a particular area, constrained by geographical formations, shows how the problem of feeding a family in ways suited to the locality can be dealt with creatively.

In this book we celebrate a few of the items that have been provided in the English kitchen for the English table.

CHAPTER ONE

THE ENGLISH KITCHEN

Tom Jaine

It is a reasonable presumption that there is something we can call 'English cookery'. However, its identity is a matter of infinite and, some say, tedious debate. There are modern commentators who both malign English cookery and imply it does not exist – that by dint of its derivative and imitative character it has lost all claim to discrete identity. This is of course absurd. If English people cook, the product must be English cookery. There are other observers, perhaps indeed a majority, that proclaim the magpie tendency of English cooks, constructing a national cuisine from the leavings of other cultures, to be the touchstone of Englishness rather than recognizing a self-reliant, indigenous tradition. We have indeed always been open to foreign influence, but which European country has not? The Germans and Dutch took as much from French cookery as we did; medieval Italians took from the Arabs in Sicily; and the French of the Renaissance took from the Italians. That we should have taken the odd chutney and curry from the Orient was only to be expected.

I distrust this characterization of English cookery for its political and philosophical undertones. We are a liberal and tolerant nation, therefore we are happy to take in the products of other cultures. This does not explain the fact that the most enthusiastic English consumers of chicken vindaloo seem to be the least tolerant and liberal sections of our society. Nor does it get to grips with the fact that, per capita, Holland has as many Chinese restaurants as Britain.

Another misbegotten, or not very helpful, means of approach to the identity of English cookery is to explore the self-evident fact that it is not French, Spanish, Italian, Greek, Arab, Chinese or some other nation's cuisine. Although such a series of negatives can be used constructively, for example by Elizabethan politicians anxious to put in place a sense of patriotic distinction – we are not Papists, and so forth – when we use this measure with reference to cookery it usually brings with it such a pantechnicon of prejudice as to raise the hackles. It is the norm that a person who states that English cookery is not like French or Italian actually means English cookery is not as good as these. That English cooks do not have the foreigners' matter-of-fact yet quality-conscious approach to raw materials. That English people do not sit down to meals in as sophisticated a way as our Continental cousins. In other words, that we are slobs, and fat and starch-laden slobs at that. Very rarely are these comparisons made between the English and German, English and Dutch or English and Scandinavian cuisines. In the first place, because most commentators know nothing of them, in the second, because they would not bear the ideological loads required of them.

Many of the problems which arise from analyses of this type are due to their ignoring the cycles of each nation's development. In this, they bear comparison with our inability to ever reach the ideal moment before joining the Euro. We constantly study the economic runes to gauge whether we have achieved the five preconditions, but our respective cycles seem always at odds. It is the same at table. Just as we here in Britain appear to follow tendencies first noticed in the United States – fast food, a greater slice of the national income spent on meals outside the home, absorption of tropical foodstuffs into the national larder – so the countries of southern Europe in particular have gradually abandoned characteristics of an earlier social and economic dispensation to align themselves more closely with the consequences of urbanization and industrialization that have been felt for many decades (indeed, in our case, centuries) in the north. The Slow Food movement may appear to be a resistance to foreign influence; in fact it is a cry for a return to a golden age destroyed by domestic Italian hands.

Whether our skill at the stove is more or less than our neighbours' is immaterial. What should be celebrated is its difference. While searching for a national identity, critics often fail to compare like with like. A peasant fresh from killing his pig at Martinmas is not the same creature, economically, intellectually or socially, as a steel-worker tired and hungry at the end of a twelve-hour shift. The assessment of our indigenous cooking is bedevilled by another, more deep-seated fallacy, that we owe everything that's any good in our cookery to France, and that because our restaurants are not as good as those on the other side of the Channel, we are merely a pale and inadequate reflection of our masters.

An historical document of lasting interest is a record by a Northampton-shire gentleman of dinners he consumed at home and at his neighbours' in the last years of the eighteenth century. Many people have kept such memoranda, of sometimes just their own catering (to avoid serving a guest the same thing twice), others of everything they ate out and about (for the purposes of self-improvement perhaps, or reporting back to the home base). Most of the meals that my Midland gentleman was served were good upper-middle-class fare: a turbot here, a goose there, a whole dinner of offal on one occasion. Nothing too grandiose, nothing too complex, but nothing too impoverished either. There was a single exception: a formal dinner given by the Earl Spencer at Althorp Park to drum up support for the family's interest during a parliamentary election. This was in three courses, with decorative pyramids and centrepieces, and with a succession of made-dishes with incomprehensible names scattered across the board. In short, it was a dinner in the French manner, doubtless cooked by a Frenchman, which showed class differences between the gentry and aristocracy at least as significant, if not as dangerous, as those between the bourgeoisie and proletariat.

Since the beginning of the seventeenth century, when that hyper-English cook Robert May was sent by his employer to learn his trade in Paris, the influence of France on upper-class British cookery has been pervasive. It has also engendered a dreadful cultural cringe on our part. Putting to one side the question of quality or gastronomic achievement, the French style of cookery had a close functional relationship with the French style of aristocratic and court-based life. The two were compatible and well adjusted. It stood to reason, therefore, that as the political and cultural influence of France on the courts and countries of Europe overtook that of its rivals, for instance that of Spain, so too would the style of its kitchens. Clients and admirers bought the whole Gallic package: architecture, furnishings, fashions and ragouts – these were fellow-travellers of absolutism, divine right and centralization.

By dint of employing French practitioners in English kitchens, our own aristocracy made a fair fist of imitation. However, as we go further down the social scale, emulation was by no means as successful. And as the links became ever more tenuous, stretched as they were by time and further social spread, so our imitations became more ridiculous – as they undeniably were by the end of the nineteenth century.

The connection between French aristocratic cookery and French restaurants is very close. Both demanded the same organization of the kitchen, both responded to the same demands of immediate production and variety. One of the Achilles heels of English culinary skills is the restaurant. This is because it is the public face of cookery, and all too often the whipping boy. Unfortunately, it is not an indigenous form at all and is ill-suited for the display of specifically English culinary characteristics. What it does best is French, because it is a French creation. Hence, to condemn English cookery as bad on the strength of its restaurants is about as pointless as condemning English cookery as ham-fisted on the grounds that its Indian restaurants have never equalled the curries of Kerala or the Punjab. We would not expect them to. However, if we penetrate the kitchens of right-thinking English households, there we will find – and have always found – matchless skill, delectable flavours, and fine cooking.

Some of the questions surrounding the identity of English cookery resurface when it comes to discussing English, or more reasonably, British regions. An arrow that is often withdrawn from the quiver of criticisms of our cooking is aimed at the fact that we do not have the regional differences that are familiar to students of French, Italian or Spanish cuisine. The first necessity is once again to compare like with like. England is a small country. France and Spain are vast. The length of Italy straddles very disparate latitudes. England has benefited from racial and religious homogeneity as well as a successful and centralized political organization. Its units of administration, the shire counties, are relatively small by contrast to the regions of France or Spain. All these things militate against too great a regional variety in the first instance. How can Dorset be held up against the Perigord, for example?

However, things look quite different if you extend the comparison to take in the whole of Britain. There is as pronounced a regional identity to the Britain which comprises England, Scotland, Wales and Ireland as there is to any Continental state. And this is as true in the kitchen as in the rest of life.

Is further subdivision possible in a small country where so much of daily life has been blanketed by a mantle of uniformity as communications break down barriers between one district and the next; education and economic activity have similar effects; and the sheer mobility of the population, up and down the social classes, and from one area to another have eroded local differences? Regionalism, in a country the size of England, comes close to parochialism.

Whatever the truth of these comments, statistics, demographics, sociology, and market analysis recognize important differences between areas, districts, or regions in England. Tastes are not the same, and they vary from place to place as well as from income bracket to income bracket. Beer, tobacco, housing, furnishings, motor vehicles, sweets and confectionery: all are subject to regional preference; why not, therefore, food and cookery?

A century ago, it was axiomatic that if two families sat down to a meal on the same day but in two distinct regions, their food would be different. Variation would extend to methods of cookery, fats and cooking mediums, staple ingredients, the structure of the meal itself, and preferred dishes. As one went up the social scale, these differences would probably reduce, as lifestyles melded into a common standard disseminated by court, capital city and university. Equally, going down the scale to the underclass, poverty and destitution would inhibit the exercise of choice. But it would be true for the middling sort – which compares, a little at any rate, with the regionalism of French bourgeois cooking.

In the intervening years, these differences have been eroded. Other influences on diet have been brought to bear: travel, education, literacy and the diffusion of information through the press, film and broadcasting. But if we are to avoid the paradox of reducing choice through extending the range of our culture – which causes the decline of pockets of variation in pursuit of new, but common horizons – we need to rediscover a sense of place, or locality.

So much good work has already been done on this subject by contributors to the Leeds Symposia, that I hesitate to make some suggestions drawing on my experience further south. The six counties of Gloucestershire, Somerset, Wiltshire, Dorset, Devon and Cornwall constitute the South Western Region defined by the Registrar General and other government agencies. It takes in several geological types, and contains variations in history and human geography that encourage some parts to look to other groupings of counties or population centres, but there are the foundations of a common style of food and cookery.

A litany of particular dishes is one way to define a regional cuisine, but it needs more than that to achieve coherence. The accidents of individual recipes need to draw on shared ingredients and approaches to cooking. To make an analogy with architecture: that houses are built from the same materials, or conform to the same principles of structure, is more important than the incidentals of surface design, for example the shape of window panes. For a culinary parallel, think of south-western France. Geese and ducks give the region its special identity. Their by-products (fat, innards, and foie gras) provide a structure for a self-contained style of cookery; the birds themselves are important ingredients; and shared methods of cooking (the confit for example) unite one community with another.

The West Country has a common medium, and significant mainstay ingredients that inform and reach out to the furthest corners of everyday cooking. The dairy farming and pasturage of the South West give beef on the one hand but more importantly milk, butter, cheese, cream and clotted cream to provide a medium (butter), a vital added ingredient (clotted cream), a staple of everyday diet (cheese) and by-products that support further regional specialization (whey for pig farmers). Thus agriculture and cookery are locked into a single cycle.

Another specialization has extended its influence into the whole spectrum of cookery: orchards and cider production. Although beer has its place (I think especially of the white ales of South Devon recorded from early modern times), cider has provided a distinctively regional drink, its own commercial infrastructure for public sale (the infamous cider houses), and a flavouring for cookery – as well as being another pillar of the diet of pigs who can gorge on windfalls in the orchards or be fed the pomace or pulp from the cider press. Eating- and cooking-apples have influenced diet and recipes in their turn.

Fish should count as much as the dairy industry towards defining a regional cuisine – from the latter day speciality of smoked mackerel, to the breeds that are found, or have been caught in earlier years, in our waters. Brill, pilchards, elvers, lampreys, mullet, hake, mackerel and sprats might be thought regional; the south west lands more crab than any other area of Great Britain; scallops, mussels and oysters are long-standing favourites; and there are several important salmon rivers.

The three groups of ingredients I have listed permeate more than just a few dishes. They contribute to a daily reality. That other parts of the country have also adopted them does not disguise their regional origin.

Perhaps less widespread in their influence, but none the less excellent and worth celebrating, are individual ingredients found or grown in the region from a comparatively early stage in our development. Among many I could cite saffron, cabbages in Paignton, broccoli and cauliflower on the south coast, Wiltshire crayfish, rock samphire and laver, seakale (first domesticated in south Devon), port wine that developed out of the Newfoundland fishery trade, salt cod from the same, and the products of the pig found throughout north Wiltshire. If you take these several items as a whole, it could be strenuously maintained that only the South West can produce this particular combination – a reasonable test of regional identity.

The mask does not slip when it comes to specific recipes and ways of cooking. There does seem an identifiable preference for cooking pies, from the pasty – a pie with an historical function – to the squab pie in several variations (pork or mutton and apples), apple pies in Dorset and Devon, or the lamprey pie sent annually to the monarch by the Corporation of Gloucester. There are also recipes that are specific to the area: Chudleighs or Cornish splits, saffron bread, Bath buns, Sally Lunns, Bath chaps, the stargazey pie and many, many more.

The regional cookery of Great Britain is almost a lost cause for several reasons. So great have been the social and cultural changes of the last century that revival smacks almost of antiquarianism. How can a Bedfordshire Clanger compete against the raucous claims of Indian, Chinese, Italian, French, Mexican, Spanish and Middle Eastern influences now given daily exposure on every medium? Would it anyway suit our lifestyle, for want of a better word? English cookery is displayed with difficulty once it departs the domestic hearth. It does not sit easily in the context of a restaurant or grandiose entertaining – save for giant tea-parties. It therefore starts at a disadvantage. We have anyway lost so much, even before it was recorded. We needed a Folksong Society approach to our kitchens before it all faded away – Florence White did indeed found the English Folk Cookery Association in the 1930s, but it was perhaps too little too late.

Most important of all, in my view, is that our critics have spent too long looking at the wrong things. False comparisons have given rise to false modesty. To be modest is a virtue, but we should never blush unnecessarily.

CHAPTER TWO

WARM, COMFORTING FOOD:
SOUPS, BROTHS AND POTTAGES

Eileen White

S oup first appeared in England in the middle of the seventeenth century, and was featured in printed recipes from the early 1700s. This means the term 'soup' began to be used at this time, and the recipes came to be presented as an item in cookery books, but the dish itself has a much older pedigree.

Samuel Pepys provides a guide to the introduction of the new word. On 16 September 1665 he had 'a mess of good broth', and on 16 July 1666 'I had some broth made me to drink which I love'. On 12 May 1667 he went with his wife to a French eating-house or ordinary run by his periwig-maker Monsieur Robin; they had a mess of pottage first, followed by pigeons and beef a-la-mode. On 15 March 1668/9 he was at the Cock in Suffolk-Street 'where I never was, a great ordinary, mightily cried up', and enjoyed a good soup and a pullet. He must have praised this meal to his wife because on 12 April he returned with her, their servant girl and two friends, 'my wife having a great desire to eat of their Soup made of pease – and dined very well'.[1] This cannot be used as a simple example of the shift of terms in a four-year period. He had broth in 1666 following a bout of indigestion, having drunk milk on top of beer, and light broths were part of invalid diets. His *potage* was taken at a French eating-house. However, 'soup' was encountered at a fashionable new ordinary, and may have been an equally fashionable new term for an old dish. Had his wife wished to make a pea soup for herself, she would not have found a recipe for it under that name in any of the contemporary published cookery books; instead she would have had to look under pottages. For example, Robert May in *The Accomplisht Cook*, first appearing in 1660, had a recipe for pease pottage.[2] Variations of this pottage, especially in its puréed or 'mushy peas' guise, go back to medieval recipes, such as that for 'Perrey of pesoun' in *The Forme of Cury* dating from around 1400.[3]

As Pepys demonstrates, the term 'soup' was being used from at least the 1660s, but it took some time to appear in print. The manuscript collections were equally conservative. Published manuscripts need to be consulted with caution. Hilary Spurling's presentation of Elinor Fettiplace's collection (dated *c.* 1604) provides a margin heading of 'Rich Almond Soup', which is the editor's title for a recipe originally given as being 'For a weake Back'. It is our modern version of the term 'soup' which is being projected back to this cure.[4] John Evelyn, Pepys' contemporary, compiled a manuscript receipt book, now published, which included pottages and broths, but no soups.[5] The manuscript compilation of Rebecca Price, *c.* 1681, has been edited as *The Compleat Cook*. There is a selection called 'Soup', but this is apparently the editor's term; the sub-heading 'all sorts of pottages, Broaths and firmity' is more likely how Rebecca Price herself would have categorized these recipes.[6] An examination of the many unpublished manuscripts in private hands and record offices around the country could provide evidence for the term 'soup' emerging into common use. Another published example, *The Receipt Book of Ann Blencowe* from 1694, has one recipe 'To make peas soope', and another 'To Make Gravysoop (from Serjeants' Inn Cook)',[7] showing that the term was used, and taken up by compilers of personal recipe collections, around the same time that it was emerging in print. This study concentrates on examples from printed works.

DEFINITIONS

The *Oxford English Dictionary* (1933) describes soup as 'A liquid food prepared by boiling, usually consisting of an extract of meat with other ingredients and seasoning', and says the word derived from the French *soupe* or sop. The *New Standard Dictionary of the English Language* (1914) says it is a 'Liquid food made by boiling meat or vegetables, or both, in water, with seasoning, and sometimes thickening; distinguished from broth, which is usually strained or free from the solid ingredients that soup retains. Soup is said to be eaten and not drunk.'

This leads to further searches, under sop, sup, sip and supper, and here the *OED* cites Old English rather than French for the derivations. A sop is a piece of bread dipped or soaked in liquid, and by extension the dish composed of soaked bread. It is also a thing of small value. To sup or sip means taking liquid or semi-liquid food in small mouthfuls, and sup in Scottish dialect means to eat with a spoon. This reflects a certain daintiness: soup is taken in small portions, just as solid food is, and so there is a link to eating as opposed to quaffing large draughts of liquid such as ale. Soup can be associated with a civilized way of eating.

Soups are found throughout the Continent: French *soupe*, Italian *zuppa* and Dutch *soop*. The two forms of spelling when the word was first adopted into English to refer to a particular dish were 'soupe' and 'soop': possibly this could relate to the French style brought by the returning monarch Charles II and the Dutch origins of his later successor William of Orange. Philologists can continue to enjoy seeking the origins of words, but here the concern is with an item of food: soup, under whatever name, in the English kitchen. The following survey is intended as a framework to examine the evolution of the dish.[8]

POTTAGES, BROTHS AND BOILED MEATS IN THE SEVENTEENTH CENTURY

There is a natural grouping of dishes in those cookery books where the authors have presented their recipes in an orderly fashion. The early compilation Harleian MS 279 (*c.*1430-40) is divided into 'Potages dyuers' (eaten with a spoon), 'Leche Metys' (which can be sliced and eaten held in the hand), and 'bake metis' (cooked in an oven, usually in a pastry case).

Gervase Markham in *The English Housewife*, first published in 1615, has a section 'Of boyled meates ordinary', made up of pottages, broths, boiled meats and stewed meats. Robert May starts his book with boiled meats, which includes hashes and pottages. Chapter VI in *The Whole Body of Cookery Dissected* by William Rabisha (1671) is devoted to strong broths and pottages, and Chapter VII to boiled meats of flesh.

The basis of all these dishes is a good broth, usually made by boiling together a knuckle or leg of veal or beef, neck end of mutton and fowls, in various combinations. The broth could be thickened with bread, or the broth was gradually ladled over slices of bread until a jelly-like consistency was obtained.[9] Some broths were grain-based, such as barley broth. Gruels, a light morning dish or invalid food, were thickened with oatmeal.

The use of cereals links pottages with other dishes such as porridge. These in turn can be traced back to the primitive diet of cereal soaked in water, or as techniques advanced grains cooked in liquid, with plants and seeds added. Archaeological research can analyse the last meals of the people whose bodies were discovered in bog burials. The 'Iceman' discovered in the Tyrolean Alps in 1991 was found to have eaten a meal of cereals, plants and ibex meat, and another of red deer venison and cereals.[10] This looks forward to the frumenty and venison that often began a medieval feast.

Pottages, by definition, are something made in a pot, and by extension something that has to be eaten with a spoon, being liquid, semi-liquid or lightly set in form. Recipes for pottages and boiled meats are the sources for the later-developed soups.

Although Robert May's *The Accomplished Cook* did not appear until 1660, the author was the product of culinary practices of the later sixteenth and early seventeenth centuries. A cursory look in his chapter on pottages for fish-days seems to provide an early example of soup, for he gives recipes for soops or butter'd meats of spinage, soops of carrots and soops of artichocks, potatoes, skirrets, or parsnips. The use of the plural gives them away: they are sops, stewed vegetables served on finely carved sippets of bread. His sugar or hony sops are another example, slices of manchet or fine bread soaked with ale spiced with mace, sugar or honey and currants.[11] This is directly related to recipes from two hundred years before. 'Caboges' were cooked in a broth thickened with grated bread, and 'soupes dorye' (or golden sops) were made with payne mayne or light bread sliced and soaked in wine, and spiced with ginger, sugar, canel (cinnamon or cassia bark), cloves and mace.[12] However, these recipes do provide links with later ones for soup.

An interesting recipe can be found in John Murrell's collection, *Murrell's Two Books of Cookerie and Carving*,[13] 'To boyle Chickens in soope'. The chicken was cooked in broth, with artichokes, raisins, currants, cauliflowers and marigold leaves. Bread used as a thickener was steeped in broth and verjuice, and sugar used to contrast the sharpness. It is interesting that the recipe is for chickens 'in soope', and not on sops. There are no clear instructions for serving, but similar recipes can be found from the sixteenth century onwards. Thomas Dawson included 'a Capon in White broth with almondes' in *The good huswifes Iewell* in 1596. The broth was enriched with marrow bones and wine, thickened with ground almonds and flavoured with prunes, raisins and dates: 'when it is enough serue it vppon soppes with your capon'.[14] Similar broths, flavoured and thickened and poured over the meat or fowl that had provided the broth are found throughout the seventeenth century. Robert May had a 'Stewed Broth' made with a knuckle of veal, mutton, marrow bone and a capon, with herbs, spices, oatmeal, dried fruits, wine and sugar: 'dish up your meat on finer sippits, and broth it'.[15]

These pottages, boiled meats, broths and sops were established in the English kitchen well before the first soup recipes appeared in print. They are to be found in Gervase Markham's *The English Housewife*, in editions from 1615 to 1683, and Hannah Wolley in the 1670s was still publishing recipes that relate back to those from a hundred years earlier.[16] Meanwhile, the professional cooks from the Restoration onwards were working away in royal and aristocratic kitchens, and in public eating houses and inns, taking in continental influences and adapting old dishes. Their recipes eventually appeared in print in the early years of the new century, and with these publications came soup.

SOUP IN THE EIGHTEENTH CENTURY

William Salmon compiled *The Family Dictionary or household companion* in 1696, and included several broths and pottages. By the fourth edition, which appeared in 1710, with additions, he had added a new section of

'Soop Brown, Soop Good, Soop White, Soop or Pease-Porridge and Soop'. He was not a cook, and has even been described as a quack-doctor.[17] Henry Howard, however, was a professional cook, registered as a Free Cook of London and working for the aristocracy. He brought out *England's Newest Way in all Sorts of Cookery* in 1703, and included as a group white soop, brown soop, good soop, white broth, pease soop, pease pottage and plumb pottage.[18] Together, these form one strand – 'soop' – of the English traditional soups.

Another strand – 'soupe' – can be found in Patrick Lamb's *Royal Cookery; or, the Complete Court-Cook*, published in 1710 after his death. He had worked for nearly fifty years in the kitchens of Charles II, James II, William and Mary, and Queen Anne. This edition contained eighteen soups: soupe santé, the French and English ways; soupe malgré and white malgré soupe (maigre, meagre or fish-day soups), two 'Soupe Borswoy' (bourgeoise); turnep soup; soupe of savoy or cabbage; soupe vermicelly (with reference to rice broth); soup Lorraine; five fish and shell fish soups; and soup profitrollé. He also inserted a bisque of pigeons, which is similar to the other soups. These recipes were presented at the beginning of the book; the 1716 edition, enlarged, was presented alphabetically, so the soups come later, with the addition of a soup-julienne.[19]

A stronger French flavour was added by Vincent La Chapelle, who worked in England for Lord Chesterfield at the time his book came out, in English, in 1733, and then for the Prince of Orange. *The Modern Cook* has recipes for Pottages – *potages* – rather than 'soups', but they are served in a 'Soop dish'. His recipe 'To make Broth' begins 'For all sorts of Soop take a leg of Beef ...'[20]

These two strands were repeated, sometimes word for word, by other compilers such as John Nott in *The Cook's and Confectioner's Dictionary* of 1723. *The Whole Duty of a Woman* (1737) in the first chapter of the cookery section, 'Of Gravies, Soups, Broths and Pottages', repeats many of the recipes already found in Lamb and La Chapelle. They were still being repeated by Martha Bradley, *c.* 1756, in *The British Housewife*.[21] Gradually, the spelling of soop and soupe became the familiar soup.

These 'new' soups were, basically, a broth thickened and flavoured and served poured over either the meat that had provided the broth, or over a separately roasted or cooked fowl, or over a French roll placed in the middle of the dish. As such, they were not so different from the seventeenth-century pottages and broths. Soup was a new name rather than a new dish, but having acquired a new name it developed new characteristics.

Lady Grisell Baillie recorded the menus of meals she had eaten, both as hostess and guest, between 1715 and 1732, so here it is possible to see what was actually eaten. She noted: pea soup and soup with peas; plum potage (a Christmas dish, associated with soups); broth, barley broth and Scots broth; soup; soup with a fowl; green soup and green soup, veal in it; brown soup; white soup and white soup with herbs; and a soup with marrowbone. All these relate to the soups already mentioned. In August 1718, at Lord Sunderland's, she had 'Soup without anything in it'.[22] This shows soup being served just as a liquid, and not with a large centrepiece of a fowl or French loaf. An example of a clear soup can be found later in the century, in Elizabeth Raffald's *The experienced English house-keeper* of 1769. For her transparent soup, the liquid was strained from the veal, herbs, mace and beaten almonds that provided the broth, and allowed to settle; it was then poured off from the sediment, and served with rice or vermicelli.[23]

EATING SOUP

Changes in recipes and table presentation that are perceptible in eighteenth-century cookery books relate to the adoption of knives and forks for eating, rather than knife and fingers. This defined how food could be prepared and served. Soups, like the earlier broths, pottages and boiled meats, continued to be served at the beginning of the meal, to be eaten with a spoon.[24] By the eighteenth century, it was customary to place the soup along with other dishes of the first course; once the soup was served, the dish was removed and a fish dish set in its place. Usually the soup was set at the top end of the table, but if there were two soups, a white and a brown for example, they were put at top and bottom. Sometimes, when there was no remove, the soup was placed in the middle of the table.[25]

Recipes from the seventeenth and eighteenth centuries provide some hints about how the pottages and soups were presented and eaten. John Murrell gave instructions 'to boyle Chickens, for one that is sicke, and to provoke sleepe'. The chicken was cooked with mace, raisins, lettuce and lemon juice, and thickened with the crust of a manchet or light bread: 'Let him drinke the broth, and eate the Lettice with the Chickens'.[26] This is diet for the sick, but it indicates the two processes of consuming a pottage, or a soup, served with a fowl.

The broth used in preparing the complicated dish of a Spanish olio was taken separately from the meat. *The Compleat Cook* (1665) suggested 'To do well, the Broth is rather to be drunk out of a Porringer, than to be eaten with a spoon though you add some small slices of bread to it, you will like it the worse'. A similar, if more refined, version was given by La Chapelle and repeated in *The Whole Duty of a Woman* in the 1730s: 'You serve it in cover'd China Cups, with slices of toasted Bread as big as your two Fingers; fill each Cup with Broth, and put a Toast at their sides. Take care your Broth be well relish'd; and serve it as hot as you can'. These consommé cups were popular on the Continent; in England they were seen more as custard cups.[27]

Patrick Lamb's soupe of savoy or cabbage was served with a duck or pigeon in the centre, and the quartered savoys around: 'There must be Room betwixt each piece of Savoy to take up Soupe with a large Spoon'.[28] Although the soup was served as a broth over the meat, the liquid seems to have been consumed separately. In presenting soup it was the liquid that was important and defined the dish; the olio was presented with only a little broth as the combination of meats was the important part. Martha Bradley explained the difference in her recipe for a Spanish olio (*c.* 1756): 'Remember it is not a Soup, but an Olio, the Things are to be eaten in Preference of the Liquor.'[29]

Another definition of soup as it developed in the eighteenth century can be found in Elizabeth Raffald's *Experienced English house-keeper* of 1769, in a recipe for ox-cheek soup:

> if you would have it eat like soup, strain and take out the meat and other ingredients, and put in the white part of a head of celery cut in small pieces, with a little browning, to make it a fine colour; take two ounces of vermicelli, give it a scald in the soup and put the top of a French roll in the middle of a tureen, and serve it up.
>
> If you wold have it eat like stew, take up the face as whole as possible, and have ready cut in square pieces a boiled turnip and carrot, a slice of bread toasted, and cut in small dices, put in a little Cayenne pepper, and strain the soup through a hair sieve upon the meat, carrot, turnip, and bread so serve it up.[30]

'Stew' had earlier been used as a verb, in recipe titles, 'to stew', or as an adjective, 'stewed'. Now it became a noun, a dish in its own right, but it was very close to the pottages and early soups in appearance. Soup became the broth strained from the meat that flavoured it, and was served here like the transparent soup, with vermicelli. The liquid element of the pottage, soop or soupe took the name of soup, and stimulated further variations.

THE LATER EIGHTEENTH CENTURY

Throughout the eighteenth century, it continued to be usual for the soup to be served poured over a fowl, meat or a French roll. The roll, whole or sliced as sops, was almost obligatory. Martha Bradley's 'Pea Soup called Puree' instructed: 'if it be to go up plain pour in the Soup without any Thing more. This is the common Way in some Families, but the Inventors of this Dish always put something substantial in the Middle.'[31] La Chapelle had a 'Crust with Mushrooms' in his pottage section which called for 'a round Soup-loaf of about a Pound Weight',[32] which suggests the size of such centrepiece. However, in other examples the soup was apparently served with nothing else in the dish. Hannah Glasse had a 'Soup Meager' which was simply poured into the soup-dish and sent to table, and an almond soup was similarly poured straight into the dish.[33]

There were more examples of soups being sieved or puréed, or thickened with a flour-butter roux as well as with eggs or grated bread. They could also be served with fried or dried bread.

Richard Briggs, in *The English Art of Cookery* (1788), included the standards from the beginning of the century, but he added many more varieties that had accumulated since then, such as onion, turtle, mock turtle, macaroni, chestnut, rice and portable soups, veal and beef broth, Scotch barley broth and examples of plum porridge and common plum porridge for Christmas. Some soups were served in the traditional way, over the fowl or meat in a dish, with garnishes round the rim, but he also illustrates another method of serving. For milk soup, thickened with almonds, he instructed: 'cut some slices of French bread, and crisp them before the fire, put them into a soup-dish or tureen, and pour the soup over them.' An onion soup and a mutton broth were also poured into tureens.[34]

SOUP IN THE NINETEENTH CENTURY

It is only possible here to hop and skip through the nineteenth century, using a few authors to illustrate various trends in the making and presentation of soup. In the second decade of the century, John Armstrong's title *The Young Woman's Guide to Virtue, Economy and Happiness … with a Complete and Elegant System of Domestic Cookery* sets the tone. His Scotch broth still echoed the old system, using a broth made with knuckles of veal, lean beef, neck of mutton and vegetables: 'When sufficiently stewed, serve up along with the meat.' Others represent the sieved purées, like carrot soup; the carrots were stewed in a broth made from beef bones and a leg of mutton, and rubbed through a sieve or coarse cloth with wooden spoons.[35]

Eliza Acton, who first published *Modern Cookery for Private Families* in 1845, followed a common practice in putting her chapter on soup at the beginning of the book, with sixty-three recipes. It begins with a list of thirty-seven ingredients that could be used in soups, ranging through meats, fowls, vegetables, grains and pastas. She provides examples of the influence of the British colonies on food in England, with a recipe for mullagatawny soup, which included curry powder, pickled mango and cocoa-nut. A footnote was added concerning this last item: 'That our readers to whom this ingredient in soups is new, may not be misled, we must repeat here, that although the cocoa-nut when it is young and fresh imparts a peculiarly rich flavour to any preparation, it is not liked by all eaters, and is better omitted when the taste of a party is not known, and only one soup is served.' Soups were thickened with flour, rice flour, arrowroot or breadcrumbs. They were not invariably served poured over bread sops, but fried bread (in other words, croutons) were served separately, for example with the 'Rich Peas Soup': 'send the soup quickly to table with a dish of small fried or toasted sippets.' She suggested the use of prepared relishes, such as curry powder. Captain White's curry paste was used in Buchanan carrot soup and cheap rice soup, and Harvey's Sauce in cheap clear gravy soups, sago soup and brown rabbit soup.[36]

Many of these trends first appeared in the eighteenth century, but the mass-produced relishes were a feature of the nineteenth-century kitchen, and some writers coloured their brown soups with caramel rather than prepare gravy from first principles.

Anne Bowman provided examples of other nineteenth-century themes in *The New Cookery Book*: 'Setting aside the consideration of economy, to begin dinner with a light soup is decidedly wholesome, and serves to avert the danger of eating too heavy a meal of solid meat, for it is an error for any one to fancy that when he has eaten heartily of roast beef only, he has necessarily made a wholesome dinner. A plate of thin soup, followed by a single slice of meat or pudding, will digest sooner and cost as little, and will conduce more to the comfort and enjoyment of life.' This illustrates both the concern for economy and the moral tone that was imparted by many writers, even for the service of soup. Anne Bowman also confirms the move away from the old style of serving, in 'A cheap Family White Soup'. The broth was based on a knuckle of veal with ham or bacon; 'then take out the veal, which can be served separately with egg or parsley sauce, and strain the soup.' The soup was thickened with arrowroot mixed with a little cream, and served with sippets of bread.[37]

The fame of Mrs Beeton – preserved in a variety of editions going far beyond the 1861 volume she edited – makes her an obvious representative of nineteenth-century cookery. Here, she stands for the laudable provision of Soup for the Poor, which featured in many of the cookery books. In *Beeton's Book of Household Management* is a 'Useful Soup for Benevolent Purposes' which the editress herself made in the winter of 1858, 8 or 9 gallons a week. It was made with ox-cheek, beef trimmings, bones, onions, leeks, herbs, celery, carrots, turnips, brown sugar, beer, rice or pearl barley, salt and pepper: 'she has reason to believe that the soup was very much liked, and gave the number of those families, a dish of warm, comforting food, in place of the cold meat and piece of bread which form, with too many cottagers, their usual meal.'[38]

It would be possible to trace the further development of soup by consulting the on-going series of volumes produced in the name of Mrs Beeton into the twentieth century, but this survey ends with the next generation, and *Mrs. A.B. Marshall's Cookery Book*. Following an established trend, the recipes are given French sub-titles. There is further use of ready-made ingredients, such as Robinson's 'Patent' Barley, and 'Patent' Groats, and her own curry powder. The endpapers of the copy consulted contain advertisments for Lemco (a meat extract or gravy substitute), Fry's Breakfast Cocoa and Bovril. Mrs Marshall also marks the severance of the soup from the meat which provided the broth: 'In the selection of the soups, care should be taken that they do not consist of anything which will be repeated in the dinner; for instance, a purée of chicken would be very bad if chickens are to be served later on.'

From the early broths and pottages to the varieties evolved under the name of soup, this dish is important to the English kitchen. Coming first on the menu, it can make or break reputations, as Mrs Marshall advised:[39]

> Among the whole of the courses of a dinner there is none which needs more attention than the soups, nor one which will show the liberality and hospitality of the house to greater advantage or disadvantage.

This has been a brief survey of the progress of pottage, soop, soupe and soup through the English cookery books, and more detailed examination would reveal more of both conservative practices and new horizons. A small bowl of soup can contain history, changes in taste, influences and innovations in the English kitchen.

SOUP RECIPES

TO BOILE A CAPON IN WHITE BROTH WITH ALMONDES.

Take your Capon with marie bones and set them on the fire, and when they be cleane skummed take the fattest of the broth, and put it in a little pot with a good deale of marie, prunes, raisons, dates whole maces, & a pinte of white wine, then blanch your almondes and strain them, with them thicken your potte & let it seeth a good while and when it is enough serue it vppon soppes with your capon.

Thomas Dawson, *The good huswifes Iewell* (1596), f. 5v.

CHESNUT SOUP.

Take half a hundred of chesnuts and notch them, put them in an earthen pan, and put them in a hot oven for half an hour, or roast them over a slow fire in an iron pan, (but mind they do not burn) peel them, and stew them one hour in a quart of veal or beef broth: in the mean time take three or four rashers of lean ham or bacon and put them at the bottom of a stew-pan, one pound of veal, one pound of lean beef, a pigeon cut into pieces, two onions stuck with cloves, and two blades of mace, a bundle of sweet herbs over the ham, with half a pint of water; sweat it gently till it sticks, but must not burn, pour in two quarts of boiling water, and skim it well; stuff two pigeons with force-meat, and stew them in the soup till tender; then take the pigeons out, and strain the soup to the chesnuts, season it with pepper and salt to your palate, and boil it up for five minutes; put the pigeons into a soup-dish, the chesnuts round them, and pour your soup boiling hot over them, and two or three pieces of crispt French bread at the top; garnish the edge of the dish with some of the chesnuts split in two.

Richard Briggs, *The English Art of Cookery* (1788), p. 46.

CLEAR MULLAGATAWNY SOUP.

Cut four large peeled onions and two sour apples in very thin slices, and put them into a stewpan with two ounces of butter and a bunch of herbs, such as thyme, parsley, and bayleaf; fry for fifteen to twenty minutes; then mix with them a tablespoonful of Marshall's curry powder, a tablespoonful of chutney, six cardomoms, two Jamaica peppercorns pounded, two ounces of glaze, a saltspoonful of coralline pepper, six pints of good stock, and any roast game or poultry bones; bring to the boil, then skim and allow the stock to cool gently for about one hour; then strain and remove the fat, and clarify; strain off through a clean soup cloth, and return to the bain marie to get hot; then serve with little round pieces of cooked game or poultry in the tureen, and have plainly boiled rice handed on a plate.

Mrs. A.B. Marshall's Cookery Book (revised ed., *c.* 1888), p. 59.

NOTES

1. Robert Latham and William Mathews, eds., *The Diary of Samuel Pepys* (London: G. Bell & Sons, 1970–77), Vols 6, p. 227; 7, p. 208; 8, p. 211; 9, pp. 483 and 516.

2. Robert May, *The Accomplisht Cook* (1660); see the facsimile of the 1685 edition, edited by Alan Davidson, Marcus Bell and Tom Jaine (Blackawton: Prospect Books, 1994), p. 421, in Section XX, 'To make all manner of Pottages for Fish-Days'.

3. Constance B. Hieatt and Sharon Butler, eds., *Curye on Inglysch* (OUP: Early English Text Society SS.8, 1985), p. 114.

4. Hilary Spurling, *Elinor Fettiplace's Receipt Book* (London: The Salamander Press, 1986), p. 192.

5. Christopher Driver, ed., *John Evelyn, Cook* (Blackawton: Prospect Books, 1997).

6. Madeleine Masson, ed., *The Compleat Cook* (London: Routledge & Kegan Paul, 1974), pp. 51–58.

7. *The Receipt Book of Ann Blencowe, A.D. 1694*, introduced by George Saintsbury (London: Guy Chapman, 1925), pp. 8 and 24.

8. For a compilation of soup recipes from 600 years, see Eileen White, *Soup* (Blackawton: Prospect Books, 2003).

9. See 'Concerning Potages' in *The Closet of Sir Kenelm Digby Opened*, edited by Jane Stevenson and Peter Davidson (Blackawton: Prospect Books, 1997), pp. 99–100. The book was originally published in 1669.

10. *The Times*, 17 September 2002. For an introduction to primitive diet, see Chapter 6, Cereals, potherbs and pottages, in C. Anne Wilson, *Food and Drink in Britain* (London: Constable & Co., 1973), pp. 186–193.

11. Robert May, pp. 426 and 423.

12. Thomas Austin, ed., *Two Fifteenth-Century Cookery-Books* (London: Early English Text Society, O.S. 91, 1888), Harleian MS 279, pp. 6 and 7.

13. John Murrell, *Murrels Two Books of Cookerie and Carving* (London: 5th edition, 1638), pp. 63–64. His *New Book of Cookerie* was first published in 1617, and the preface to the *Two Books* is dated 1630. The 1638 edition was published in facsimile by Jacksons of Ilkley (1985).

14. Thomas Dawson, *The good huswifes Iewell* (London: new edition with additions, 1596), f. 5v. The two parts of *The Good Huswifes Jewell* of 1596/7 were published in facsimile by Theatrum Orbis Terrarum, Amsterdam, 1977.

15. Robert May, pp. 14–15.

16. For editions of *The English Housewife*, see F.N.L. Poynter, *A Bibliography of Gervase Markham 1568?–1637* (Oxford: The Oxford Bibliographical Society, 1962). Hannah Wolley, *The Queen-like Closet or Rich Cabinet* (London: 2nd edition, 1672).

17. William Salmon, *The Family Dictionary or Household Companion* (London: 1696; 4th edition, 1710). The 1710 Soop recipes are on pp. 467–8. See his entry in the *Dictionary of National Biography*, 1897 edition).

18. Henry Howard, *England's Newest way in all sorts of Cookery, Pastry, and all Pickles that are fit to be Used* (London: first edition 1703; the edition consulted was the 3rd edition of 1710), pp. 33–37. Good Soop was made using a broth prepared with a leg of beef, a knuckle of veal, a neck of mutton and a crust of bread; it was then strained off. White wine, herbs and spinach were added to the broth, which was used to boil a hen. The hen was served on sippets of bread, along with the broth thickened with orange juice and egg yolks.

19. Patrick Lamb, *Royal Cookery; or the Complete Court-cook* (London: 1710), pp. 1–29; (2nd edition, 1716), pp. 260–274.

20. Vincent La Chapelle, *The Modern Cook* (London: 3 volumes, 1733; the edition consulted was the 2nd, 1736), pp. 1–80. As well as Pottages, this section includes Olios, Bisques, a

Bain-Marie, Broths, Waters, physical broths and a 'Pottage enough for fifty Poor for a little Money'.

21. John Nott, *The Cook's and Confectioner's Dictionary: Or, the Accomplish'd Housewife's Companion* (London: 1723). *The Whole Duty of a Woman: Or, an Infallible Guide to the Fair Sex* (London: 1737); Chapter XV, of Gravies, Soups, Broths and Pottages, pp. 177–219. Martha Bradley, *The British Housewife: Or, the Cook's, Housekeeper's. and Gardiner's Companion* (London: 1756–1758); facsimile edition (Blackawton: Prospect Books, 1996–1998).

22. Robert Scott-Moncrieff, *The Household Book of Lady Grisell Baillie 1692–1733* (Edinburgh: Edinburgh University Press and Scottish History Society, 1911) pp. 281–304.

23. Elizabeth Raffald, *The Experienced English Housekeeper* (Manchester: 1769), p. 5. A modern edition has been published with an introduction by Roy Shipperbottom (Lewes: Southover Press, 1997).

24. For examples of the place of pottages and boiled meats in formal menus from the 15th to the 17th centuries, see Constance B. Hieatt and Sharon Butler, op. cit. pp. 39–41; Thomas Austin, op.cit., pp. 57–64; Anne Ahmed, ed., *A Proper Newe Booke of Cokerye* (Cambridge: Corpus Christi College, 2002), pp. 30–41; Robert May, op. cit., Bills of Fare given in the introductory section.

25. Examples of the table layout and place of soup can be discerned in the menus of Lady Grisell Baillie, op.cit. There are many table layouts and bills of fare in the cookery books of the 18th century. A good example is in Eliza Smith, *The Compleat Housewife: or Accomplish'd Gentlewoman's Companion* (London: 1727 and editions to 1773). A facsimile of the 15th edition was produced by Literary Services and Production Limited in 1968, including both Bills of Fare for every Season of the Year, and fold-out plans of table placements.

26. John Murrell (1638), p. 90.

27. *The Compleat Cook* (London: 1655). This was part of a compilation called *The Queen's Closet Opened*. See the facsimile of the 1671 edition, *The Compleat Cook and A Queens Delight* (London: Prospect Books, 1984), pp. 92–93. La Chapelle, op.cit., pp. 3–4. *The Whole Duty of a Woman*, pp. 210–211.

28. Patrick Lamb (1710), pp. 13–14.

29. Martha Bradley, Prospect edition, Vol. III, pp. 344–345.

30. Elizabeth Raffald (1769), pp. 7–8.

31. Martha Bradley, Volume III, pp. 427–428.

32. La Chapelle, p. 50.

33. Hannah Glasse, *The Art of Cookery Made Plain and Easy* (London: 1747); facsimile edition (London: Prospect Books, 1983) pp. 76–77 and 78.

34. Richard Briggs, *The English Art of Cookery According to the Present Practice* (London: 1788), Chapter II, Soups, pp. 29–62; see especially pp. 44, 52 and 59.

35. John Armstrong, *The Young Woman's Guide to Virtue, Economy, and Happiness .. with a Complete and Elegant System of Domestic Cookery* (Newcastle upon Tyne: 4th edition, no date, *c.* 1820), see pp. 192–193 and 195.

36. Eliza Acton, *Modern Cookery for Private Families* (London: Newly Revised and much Enlarged Edition, 1856): Chapter I, Soups; examples given are on pp. 11, 14, 31–32, 35–36, 41, 44–45 and 46–47.

37. Ann Bowman, *The New Cookery Book: A Complete Manual of English and Foreign Cookery on Sound Principles of Taste and Science* (London: 2nd edition, 1869), pp. 48 and 76.

38. Isabella Beeton, ed., *Beeton's Book of Household Management* (London: 1861), pp. 84–85.

39. *Mrs. A.B. Marshall's Cookery Book* (London: Revised Edition, no date – *c.* 1888); see pp. 477–478.

CHAPTER THREE

DISTRIBUTED TO
THE POOR ON MAUNDY THURSDAY:
THE RISE AND FALL OF THE HERRING

Ann Rycraft

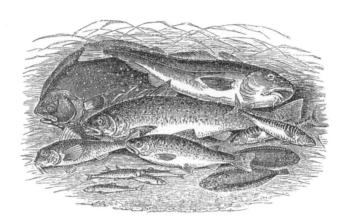

A lan Davidson wrote of the herring that it is 'of all fish probably the one which has had most influence on the economic and political history of Europe'.[1] It is remarkable that this problematic fish should have had any such influence, and have been, for some centuries, a staple part of the diet. The use of the herring as food presents three main problems.[2] First, these fish swim in enormous, closely packed, shoals; in the mid-sixteenth century, it was said that 'an axe or halberd thrust into their midst sticks firmly upright'.[3] The shoals range over the north Atlantic from Iceland southwards, and from the coasts of Holland and France westwards to North America. Their occurrence, however, fluctuates; suddenly – and bewilderingly – they will diminish in size, or fail to appear at all. It has been suggested that one of the reasons for the Vikings' voyages was that shoals had failed to appear in their waters and so they sailed south in search of them. The third problem is that the herring is a fatty fish, unlike, for example, cod. The fattiness is not excessive, but it does mean that the fish begins to deteriorate as soon as it is taken from the water. Even if a shoal, as occasionally happened, came close to land, and the fish were quickly available, slowness of transport meant that it would have been rancid before it left the port area.

English fishermen seem to have solved the problems of navigating beyond inshore waters, to reach the shoals, and of making nets strong enough to raise the fish, during the decades after the Romans withdrew, in the early years of the fifth century. Their abilities accorded well with an increased demand for fish. With Celtic Christianity holding fast in the north and Roman Christianity spreading from the south, the idea of religious fasting was developing. The growing number of religious houses, then the clergy, and eventually the laity, needed, for fast days, an alternative protein food to meat. The number of fasting days quickly grew until Wednesdays, Fridays and Saturdays, the eves of saints' days and the whole of Lent were meat-free. Freshwater fish were caught and sold; fish were kept live in the stewponds which some religious houses and noble and manorial houses possessed, but the demand, especially from the laity in the developing towns, was greater. Nothing could be done, then as now, about the fluctuations of the shoals, but increasing the number of fish landed and available for distribution was helped by the solution of the third problem. Air drying, then widely used in northern Europe for white fish, notably cod, is not suitable for the oily herring. The air-dried fish – stockfish – was sometimes salted before drying; either by experimenting with this, or by continued knowledge of a method of food preservation known in classical Rome, eventually the method of preserving herring was found to be by salting them. At first this (presumably) consisted of tipping salt over the whole fish, which would have preserved them, though not for very long; the time could be extended a little if the fish were first gutted. In the late thirteenth century a better method was developed. The fish, having been landed under salt, were soaked in brine, then hung in chimneys and well smoked.[4] It is not clear whether the fish were first gutted; perhaps this varied. The smoked herrings – 'red herrings' – were then packed tightly into barrels and ready for transport. By 1599, this process had been refined sufficiently for these fish to be described as 'large, fresh, fat, soft and pliable'.

At about the same time as this smoking process was being developed, the Dutch had begun to use an improved method of salting. The herring were gutted and well soaked in brine, before being barrelled between layers of salt, and sealed. The herring produced by this method were very salty (and towards the bottom of the barrel, disintegrating) but soft; they were 'white herring'. These two varieties of preserved herring became the staple food of fast days, supplemented (especially when herring catches were low) by the famously hard air-dried stockfish and, for those who had fishing rights, stewponds or who could afford them, freshwater fish.[5] The shoals of herring usually arrived in late spring off Shetland, and then swam down the east coasts of Scotland and England to East Anglia, and on southwards.[6] The shoals were of course no respecters of boundaries, actual or claimed; there was rivalry and dispute with the Dutch over fishing off the East Anglian and southern English coasts. The barrels of smoked or salted fish were sent inland for sale, presumably rather too late for that year's Lent, but there were the many other fasting days. If a church feast had of necessity to be held on a fasting day, then fish would be served for all courses; luxury fish (porpoise, carp, perhaps puffin) at the top tables, red and white herrings to the lower orders.[7] Preserved herrings were also, because they were usually cheap, food for the poor. Because of the quantity of fish required and the shoals' varying routes and numbers, England, as well as catching herring, imported them; salted 'white' fish, for instance, from Iceland through Bristol and both red and white herrings from Holland through Hull.[8]

In the sixteenth century, after the dissolution of the religious houses and the reformation of the Church in England, the need for fish declined. The religious houses had been major consumers. At Selby Abbey, for instance, in 1416 the kitchener accounted for 38,590 red herrings and 1,440 white herrings (in addition to 474 'salted fish' and 869 'dried fish') and for an additional 1,200 red herrings given to the poor on Maundy Thursday.[9] The Wednesday fast had already been abolished, followed by the abolition of those on Fridays, Saturdays and during Lent. The Friday and Lenten fasts had continued, however, to be to some extent observed. In 1545, in *A Proper Newe Booke of Cokerye*, there is 'a service for fish days', comprising two courses of various sorts of fish, including both red and white herring; a copy of this book probably belonged to the wife of the impeccably Protestant Archbishop Matthew Parker.[10] Later in the century, the Friday and, after that, the Saturday fast days were for a time revived. Significantly, this revival was not for religious reasons, but in order to support the fishing trade (and to keep boats and skilled men available in case of war). Still, after religious fasting had disappeared, the demand for herrings as cheap regular food continued. The trade was hit in 1643 by one of Charles I's money-raising taxes, the imposition of a duty on salt. This charge, however, provoked an advance in preserving technique. The salters had already begun to add saltpetre to salt and they now found that this, without salt, would preserve fish, and moreover that only a very small quantity was needed. Saltpetre has an added advantage, though this was not appreciated at the time; it kills, rather then merely inhibits, bacteria.

The supply of fish was diminished in 1651 by an Act under which only herring caught in British vessels could be landed in this country. However, improvements to roads in the late seventeenth and eighteenth centuries meant that such supplies as there were could be moved more quickly and safely. This increased (at least in some areas) speed in distribution encouraged the development of a new product – the cold fish pie. Gutted and boned herrings were cooked, placed in a thick pastry case (which was probably not meant to be eaten) and sealed under butter; the pie was then quickly delivered. Further improvements in landing and distribution followed. Boats were built with 'wells' or 'hatches' in which fish could be kept alive until landing. From the early nineteenth century, ice was used to keep fish fresh, first for salmon, then for other varieties. The rapid expansion of the railways during the century revolutionized distribution and, from the latter half of the century, steamboats were used for fishing, allowing quicker sailing to the shoals, a greater weight of fish to be caught and a quicker return to port. Two new cures were developed: in the early nineteenth century, the 'Yarmouth bloater' and later the 'Newcastle kipper'. Yarmouth was the main port for landing the fat, late-summer herring on their journey south; these were not gutted, but soaked for a short time in brine and then lightly smoked. Bloaters did not stay fresh for more than a few days and so were often, after smoking, made into fish paste. The kipper first appeared in London in 1846. The process, which had been developed during the 1840s by a Seahouses fish curer, was a variation of the red herring. The small early-summer herring were gutted, split down the back, lightly brined, opened out and smoked.

Nevertheless, despite these developments in fishing, transport and processing, by the beginning of the twentieth century the herring trade in England was in decline and a great deal of the catch was leaving the domestic market. Much was going as salted fish to eastern Europe, where there was (and is) a greater taste for it. Fresh fish in ice went to Germany, where it was heavily smoked to make, for example, buckling, or to be filleted, rolled and pickled ('rollmops'). Similarly, fresh iced fish went to Scandinavia and to the Low Countries to be marinated, pickled or sauced. Perhaps surprisingly, red herrings were still being produced (often smoked even more heavily, to make the stiff, dry 'black herrings') for export to Africa and the Middle East. These markets all collapsed in 1914. Between the two World Wars the Herring Industry Board was set up, to oversee the trade and, in particular, to encourage home consumption. But by this time, the catches were in serious decline, with shoals now consistently, rather than intermittently, smaller. Whether this was because of natural causes, overfishing or the development of the (especially Danish) fishmeal industry, is a matter of much debate. Certainly there had been exploitation of stocks and now the herring fleets paid a heavy price; the fishing season, fishing grounds, nets, were heavily controlled; boats were laid up and jobs lost. Herring, once so copious and cheap, are now scarce and comparatively expensive. Though they are an excellent source of protein and of the fish oil, now known to be so beneficial, fishmongers say that demand is very low. This may be because of price; but the fish does not lend itself to modern eating habits of 'snacking' or 'grazing'; there is no tradition in England (as, for example, in Holland or Denmark) of pickled herrings as snacks or as street food. The smell of cooking herring or kippers lingers in the house, and then there are the bones.... Nowadays, most people's

acquaintance with the fish – if indeed they have one – will probably be boil-in-the-bag, salty, dyed kipper fillets. Once it was so simple:

> Old Joe has gone fishing and
> Young Joe has gone fishing and
> You Know has gone fishing and
> Found them a shoal.
> Pull them in in handfuls,
> And in capfuls,
> And in panfuls.
> Bring them in sweetly,
> Gut them completely,
> Pack them up neatly,
> Sell them discreetly,
> Oh, haul away.[11]

Now, perhaps, herrings are set to be the next gourmet 'discovery'.

AN ENDNOTE ON FIGURATIVE USES OF 'RED HERRING'

A 'red herring' means an attempt to divert attention from the main question. The origin of the saying is the laying of a false trail in hunting. The first printed occurrence is in *The Hunter. A discourse of horsemanship, directing the right way to breed, keep and train a horse, for ordinary Hunting and Plates*, printed in Oxford in 1685. If the ordinary hunt has not been strenuous enough to make the horse you are training sweat thoroughly, then you lay a 'train-scent' of three or four miles by 'viz. the trailing or dragging of a dead cat or fox (or in case of necessity a Red-Herring)'. You then 'lay on your fleetest dogs [and] ride it briskly'.

'Neither flesh nor fish nor good red herring', meaning neither one thing nor the other, useless. The first printed occurrence, 1538, lacks the herring. This was added in 1546, perhaps to make the statement more emphatic – red herring is not flesh (meat) nor, in its final state, is it exactly fish; so, neither one nor the other. Another suggested origin is that flesh was food for the gentry, fish for the clergy and red herring for the rest, so anything which did not fit one of these categories was useless.

AND A CULINARY NOTE

Both herrings and kippers have a good, distinctive, taste and can be treated simply. For herring, roll the gutted, trimmed and cleaned fish in seasoned oatmeal and fry in butter, 4 or 5 minutes on each side. Eat with buttered bread. A traditional accompaniment, if you must, is white sauce flavoured with dry mustard. The best way with kippers is Jane Grigson's; put them, heads down, into a large jug and cover them completely with boiling water. Leave for about 10 minutes and drain well. If you want to be more complicated, Gervase Markham, *The English Housewife*, 1649, has a recipe for herring pie, which combines skinned, boned and boiled herrings with pears, dried fruit and spices, in a crust ornamented with candied sugar. See also J. Grigson, *Good Things*, 1971 and A. Heath, *Herrings, Bloaters and Kippers*, 1954.

NOTES

1. Alan Davidson, *The Oxford Companion to Food* (Oxford: Oxford University Press, 1999).
2. 'Herring' is here used to describe the whole species, *clupea harengus*, including the geographic, and slightly differing, populations, such as the Baltic herring.
3. Olaus Magnus, *A Description of the Northern Peoples*, 1555, trans. P. Fisher (Hakluyt Society, 1999).
4. Fish smoking (now producing kippers, rather than red herrings) is still carried out in smokehouses in the old herring ports at Craster, Northumberland, and Whitby, North Yorkshire.
5. In the late fourteenth century stockfish were said to need hitting with a mallet for a good hour, followed by soaking in warm water for 12 hours; *Le Ménagier de Paris*, ed. G.E. Brereton & J.M. Ferrier (Oxford: Clarendon Press, 1981). The price of freshwater fish is emphasized by its being given by cities to distinguished guests: see, for example, entries in the *York City Chamberlains' Account Rolls, 1396–1500*, ed. R.B. Dobson (Surtees Society 192, 1980).
6. The city of Norwich presented the sovereign with 24 pies (size not stated) made with the year's first fresh herrings. In the last century, groups of women, 'herring lasses', would travel down the coast as the shoals moved south, working in each port as skilled and fast fish gutters and packers; see also Alan Davidson, *North Atlantic Seafood* (London: Macmillan, 1979), p. 28.
7. At the enthronement feast of the Archbishop of Canterbury, William Wareham, in Lent 1504, puffins (which were thought to live in the sea and so were permitted food on fast days) were served to the top table.
8. See *The Overseas Trade of Bristol in the Later Middle Ages*, ed. E.M. Carus-Wilson (Bristol Record Society 7, 1937) and *The Customs Accounts of Hull, 1453–1490*, ed. W.R. Childs (Yorkshire Archaeological Society Record Series 144, 1986).
9. G.S. Haslop, 'A Selby kitchener's roll of the early fifteenth century', *Yorkshire Archaeological Journal*, vol. 48, 1976.
10. A copy of this book, printed probably in 1557–8, is bound into a collection of short texts, now in the Parker Library at Corpus Christi College, Cambridge, assembled by the book collector Matthew Parker, Master of the College, later Archbishop of Canterbury. It seems unlikely that the book belonged to Parker himself; more probable that its original owner was his wife Margaret.
11. M. Slater, *Peter Grimes* (libretto), 1945.

CHAPTER FOUR

BLANCMANGE:
A TALE OF SEVEN CENTURIES

C. Anne Wilson

B lancmange has been prepared in the English kitchen for well over
seven hundred years, undergoing substantial changes before it turned
into the cornflour-based confection of our childhood. I doubt
if many of today's children have ever tasted it, though the very similar
cornflour-based custard powder is still freely available in supermarkets.

Medieval blancmange was a dish for noble and well-to-do households,
since the rice, almonds and sugar that were its characteristic ingredients were
imported from the Mediterranean region, and were relatively expensive. Its
English name derived from the French *blanc mengier*, meaning white food,
but the dish itself must have reached Europe from the eastern Mediterranean
through the Crusaders, who occupied parts of Syria and Palestine for nearly
two centuries (1098–1291).

The blancmange or 'white food' of Western Europe is rooted in the cookery of the Saracens, even though no direct recipe in Arabic has yet been found. But there are other, rather similar, dishes in Western medieval cookery that acknowledge the link, for instance *blanc de Syree* (white dish of Syria) known from recipes in both Anglo-Norman French and English manuscripts; and mawmeny, which in its early period resembled the Arabic *ma'mūnïya*.[1]

Blancmange was eaten by wealthy people in most countries of Western Europe, and similar recipes exist in their cookery manuscripts under the same name in the appropriate language. The French form, '*blanc mengier*', was adapted only slightly to name the English recipe, which is usually spelt out as 'blomanger' or 'blaumanger' in manuscripts of the fourteenth and fifteenth centuries. The earliest recipes in England were, of course, written in Norman French for the use of the mastercooks of the French-speaking Court and aristocracy, and the French headings were kept on even after the recipes themselves had been translated into English.

Instructions vary slightly, but blancmange in the medieval English kitchen contained the basic ingredients of cooked capon meat or chicken breast, either ground in a mortar or teased into fine shreds, plus ground almonds sieved with water to make almond milk, and white sugar, and a starch thickener in the form of ground rice. In fifteenth-century recipes, partridge or pheasant could be an alternative to capon. These ingredients were cooked together into a dense or standing pottage. The top was decorated with blanched, fried almonds, sometimes augmented with pomegranate seeds, or a sprinkling of red or white aniseed comfits.[2] For fasting days fish blancmange was made with pounded or teased out white fish to replace the capon or chicken element.

Because of its white colour, blancmange had to be prepared with care, and kept away from disfiguring smoke and smuts. This hazard is referred to in an early fourteenth-century recipe for the rather similar white *blanc de Syree*, which requires the ingredients to be boiled in a clean small pot; and the dish itself to be 'made in a place without filth'.[3]

In English recipe collections, blancmange always appears alongside the other major pottages prepared in the kitchens of the great families. It could be served in either the first or second course, as could *blanc de Syree* (which is listed in menus rather more often). In French cookery manuscripts, however, blancmange often features among recipes specifically designated as food for the sick, due to its bland and healthy ingredients – sugar was still a health food in medieval times.

The blandness of the dish led Terence Scully to propose that the French name could originally have been *'blant mengier'* which would have been pronounced in the same way as *blanc mengier*, and would have meant 'bland food'.[4] This seems unlikely, especially in the English kitchen, where pottages with distinctive colours were popular dishes for the feasts of the aristocracy. The earliest English recipe for *blanc de Syree* is followed by ones for *vert de Syree* and *jaune de Syree*, coloured respectively green with parsley and yellow with saffron; and several other coloured pottages follow. The 'blanc' in the earliest English 'blancmange' did acknowledge the basic whiteness of the dish, even if one or two later recipes suggest adding saffron.

For decorative effect, English cooks often prepared blancmange in its own natural shade of creamy white, and then 'departed' it with another differently coloured pottage. 'Depart' originally meant 'divide', and there are French recipes for blancmange divided into as many as four parts, three coloured gold, red and blue with vegetable dyes, and the fourth left in its natural shade. All four were then served in together.[5] English cooks, to judge from their recipes, liked to 'depart' blancmange with 'caudel ferry', a yellow dish made from ground pork and capon flesh, almond milk and eggs and spiced with saffron; or alternatively with a pottage called 'sandal', of similar ingredients, but reddened by either Indian sandalwood or alkanet root. These provided a contrast to the whitish colour of the blancmange when set alongside it on the table.[6]

In the late Middle Ages blancmange acquired another ingredient that radically altered its flavour – rosewater. This distilled water first reached the West through Arab medicine, as a cooling remedy for hot diseases. But the Saracens also employed rosewater in cookery, to flavour both sweet and savoury dishes; and that usage too eventually reached Western Europe.

Rosewater appeared rarely and quite late in English cookery books, under the name 'ewrose', from contemporary French, *eau rose*. But it had already stimulated English cooks into inventing a pottage called 'rosee'. It was unique to English cuisine, and was made from the usual blancmange ingredients, flavoured and coloured with pounded red rose petals. The starch element could be rice-flour or breadcrumbs with amidon, the wheat-flour thickener. By the fifteenth century, 'rosee' was sometimes made without a meat or fish component, and was then recommended as an accompaniment to fried fish.[7]

In Tudor times rosewater entered English blancmange too, partly through the influence of Italian recipes. Platina's book of 1468, *De honesta voluptate* ('On honourable pleasure'), the earliest printed book on diet and food, was reissued many times over the next 150 years. It influenced well-educated readers all over Europe, and rosewater blancmange was among its recipes.

Platina attributes the recipe to his friend the mastercook Martino of Como, whose manuscript version survives with the heading '*Per fare biancho mangiare*'. The blancmange mixture – the usual ground almonds, ground-up breast of capon, and sugar – was boiled in a clean pot over a slow fire. 'When it is cooked,' says Platina, 'put in three ounces of rosewater' – his recognition that rosewater loses much of its fragrance to the air, if boiled with other ingredients. He suggests serving his blancmange in one large dish, or in smaller separate dishes, or alternatively dividing it and colouring one part with egg yolks and saffron.[8]

Rosewater gradually became more prominent in the cuisine of well-to-do English families. But the recipes for blancmange went into the melting-pot. That was partly due to the wider dissemination of recipes through printed books, and to the vagaries of both scribes and printers. Thus the 'Blewe Manger' recipe in *A Proper Newe Booke of Cokerye* calls for half a pound of 'rye flower' instead of 'rice flour' (the 'c' had been overlooked by someone more familiar with rye, which could be spelt with either an 'i' or a 'y' at that time). The recipe contains shredded capon meat, but omits the almonds, and requires half a gallon each of milk and cream, thus yielding a very runny pottage.[9]

The Good Huswife's Handmaid published in 1597 has more plausible instructions, with the half-pound of rice pounded, sieved, and cooked with one quart of milk, plus shredded capon meat, but still no almonds. The stages of cookery are explained carefully, and this recipe would have worked in the kitchens of the merchants, lawyers, clergy, and other comfortably-off people who bought the cookery books. In the same book another blancmange recipe suggests fine white breadcrumbs as the thickener.[10]

Nevertheless, it was the newer concept of the meatless blancmange that would go forward into the future. The sweet flower-petal pottages of the fifteenth century, thickened with ground rice, were meatless. An early attempt at blancmange without chicken or fish in *The good huswifes Iewell*, 1596, comprises a pint of cream, 12 or 15 egg yolks and sugar, and 'a little rosewater that it may taste thereof', all simmered together. A second dishful is prepared from the whites of all the eggs strained with the other ingredients.[11] Here is influence from Platina, whose capon-meat blancmange could be divided, and have one part yellowed by egg-yolks and saffron; and influence, too, from the medieval practice of 'departing' the white blancmange with a dish of another colour.

But the true way forward was foreshadowed in Lady Elinor Fettiplace's Receipt Book. This book was recopied by a scribe in 1604, but the recipes within are earlier, and her blancmange would have been Elizabethan. It requires ground rice, and ground almonds strained with 'the clearest jellie of a leg of veal', plus rosewater, sugar, ginger and cinnamon, 'and boile it a good while, and when it is cold, serve it.'[12] Jelly was to be the key to the next phase of blancmange.

For the following sixty years, blancmange went underground in England. Perhaps it was still prepared in the kitchens of ladies like Elinor Fettiplace. But it is absent from the best-selling cookery books of the period; and when Robert May published several recipes in the 1660s in *The Accomplisht Cook*, he 'modernized' some of them by suggesting that the blancmange mixture be set in shaped pastry cases similar to the multi-shaped ones he recommended for his fruit tarts. The ingredients of the blancmange itself are the traditional ones: minced capon-meat, ground almonds, rosewater and sugar. He offers fish versions too. The thickeners vary, being white breadcrumbs, rice-flour or egg-whites, alone or combined. One recipe is meatless, comprising rice-flour, cow's milk and sugar, with a flavouring of rosewater.[13] The whiteness of the basic blancmange and its consistency were both more significant characteristics than its actual ingredients.

Blancmange maintained its presence in seventeenth-century French cookery books. There is a meatless blancmange of ground almonds sieved with breadcrumbs, and flavoured with white wine, verjuice and pale spice powder, in a late edition of the *Grand Cuisinier* published in Rouen in 1620. It was made to accompany roast capon or other roast meat, or fried fish. The same recipe reappears in *L'Escole Parfaite des Officiers de Bouche* in 1662. But there it is secondary to another blancmange; and that one begins with a capon and a good calf's foot, and instructions to 'prepare them as you did for the jelly.' The jelly-broth, the cooked capon-meat minced with breadcrumbs, ground almonds, rosewater and sugar are combined, and then turned into a dish to set.[14]

The book was translated into English by Giles Rose in 1682; and blancmange came back into favour as court food in England as well as France. In both countries blancmange was becoming very closely associated with jelly, not merely through its reliance on jelly-stock, but also because the two were served side by side. Thus Nicolas de Bonnefons advised the serving of varied egg dishes, plus 'jellies of all colours and blancmanges' in the sixth course of his elaborate menu for a feast of eight courses. Blancmange appeared in similar partnership at King James II's Coronation feast in April 1685, when Patrick Lamb prepared three dozen glasses of lemon jelly and three dozen glasses of blancmange for the corners of the Queen's end of the table.[15] Jelly glasses had recently come into fashion to display coloured jelly. In this instance they showed once more the historic combination of yellow and white, representing gold and silver.

It is possible that the blancmange served at the Coronation feast was composed simply from jelly-stock, ground almonds and sugar, with a little cow's milk for extra whiteness. French cuisine was influential at the Court of King James II, and that was the blancmange recipe in the editions of La Varenne's *Le cuisinier françois* published during the 1680s.[16]

But Robert May's jelly recipes demonstrate that jellies based on calf's-foot and capon stock were already being reinforced by hartshorn or isinglass in the English kitchen. John Evelyn's instructions 'To make manger blanc' require simply hartshorn jelly combined with ground almonds and sugar, with orangeflower water for flavouring. The capon-meat or fish element has finally been abandoned, and the cereal thickener is replaced by jelly. When Patrick Lamb published his recipes in 1710, his 'blancmangé' was based on strong hartshorn jelly-stock and pounded almonds, though it had further flavouring of lemon-juice, spices and Rhenish wine.[17]

French cuisine continued to influence English cookery through the eighteenth century, working its way down from aristocratic families with their French cooks to more modest kitchens. And it was probably the French name of blancmange that helped it to survive in the English kitchen in the face of competition from two other named confections: leach and flummery.

Late medieval leach had very different ingredients, being based on pressed curds, or egg custard or various other combinations that could be sliced after cooking, and then served in slices. A pale form already being made in the fifteenth century was based on calf's foot jelly with almond milk and sugar (sometimes 'departed', with half the mixture coloured red with sandalwood). This type became known as white leach, and in the Elizabethan recipe published by Thomas Dawson it appears as a sweet milk jelly flavoured with rosewater, to be cut up into cubes that were decorated with gold leaf for special occasions. John Murrell's *New Booke of Cookerie* of 1615 has a 'white leach of almonds', set with isinglass, and thus very similar to the meatless, jellied blancmange. Murrell adds, 'If you please, you may cast some of it into colours.' He suggests yellow tinted with saffron, green with the juice of green wheat, and red with turnsole.[18] White leach stayed in the cookery books through the seventeenth and eighteenth centuries, but disappeared soon afterwards.

Flummery also turned into a sweet almond or cream jelly, having begun its career as a rather solid, slightly acid, jelly, made from the liquid drawn from oatmeal steeped in water. In Wales it was called llymru, and that name was anglicized to flummery in Cheshire and Lancashire. It became well known throughout England, especially after Gervase Markham praised it in *The English Housewife*. But before long it too, like leach and blancmange, had become a jelly set with hartshorn or isinglass; and the original flummery had to be identified thereafter as 'oatmeal flummery'.

During the eighteenth century sweet jellies, blancmanges, flummeries and white leach were all dishes for the second course of a dinner, or for a supper. All had great potential for decoration. Moulds were already in use to print designs on the thick jellies made from quince, apricot, and other fruit pulps that were prepared for the banquet. John Murrell wrote about his amber-coloured 'jellie of pippins': 'When it is cold, you may turn it out of your moulds, and it will be printed on the upper side.' In another recipe he advised that the boxes or moulds should 'be laid in water before you use them three or four hours, and the Gellie will not cleave unto them.'[19]

Robert May mentioned the use of tin or wooden moulds for setting calf's foot jellies,[20] and Peter Brears has tracked down some eighteenth-century moulds. He described them, and also supplied some beautiful drawings among the illustrations to the second part of his article, 'Transparent Pleasures', published in *Petits propos culinaires* 54 (1996). Moulds came into use for blancmanges, too, especially towards the end of the eighteenth century, when they were given the new name of 'shapes'.

Contemporary recipes quite often call for blancmange to be set in cups or small bowls, and then turned out onto a plate. Some could be coloured, so a white blancmange standing on the centre of a plate could have four others in different colours placed around it. Alternatively, ribbon blancmange could be built up in layers in a bowl or mould, sometimes with a layer of jelly included. Although the colouring agents – saffron, cochineal, etc. – were usually added after the basic mixture had been made up, occasionally a particular colour received its own recipe. An example is Elizabeth Raffald's 'green blancmange', which incorporates two ounces each of sweet and bitter almonds ground up, the juice of spinach and a spoonful of French brandy.[21]

There were other decorative uses for blancmange. Mrs Mary Eales wrote in 1718, 'Put it in a broad earthen or china Dish, and the next day, when you use it, cut it with a Jagging Iron into long slips, and lay it in Knots in the Dish or Plate you serve it up in.' Almost a hundred years later, Joseph Bell recommended that thin slabs of coloured blancmange be cut into either shreds or shapes to provide a decorative edging for larger moulded blancmanges.[22]

Playing cards were created out of flummery or blancmange to impress dinner guests (Peter Brears explains in his article how this was done). Joseph Bell's book of 1817 has a recipe headed 'Roman pavement', for which flat moulded blancmanges, some tinted pale brown with sack, others pinkish with cherry brandy, were cut into square tesserae to imitate a mosaic floor. 'Place each in an irregular manner on the shape', he wrote,' making it as high and as romantic as you can.'[23]

One colour rated special treatment, and that was yellow. Dutch flummery was based on a jelly broth with several eggs or egg yolks whisked into it. It could also include lemon zest and juice, and a quantity of wine. The recipes vary slightly, and were offered under several names: Dutch flummery, Dutch blancmange, lemon blancmange, and even the Frenchified 'jaunemange'.

Cleanliness was still a problem. Maria Rundell wrote: 'Observe to let the blancmange settle before you turn it into the forms, or the blacks will remain at the bottom of them, and be on top of the blancmange when taken out of the molds.'[24]

The flavourings changed over time, though almonds remained a constant, frequently mentioned even in nineteenth-century recipes. Rosewater continued in high fashion for 200 years, but by the 1680s orange-flower-water had become the new vogue, demanded in recipes of Rebecca Price and John Evelyn for leach and blancmange respectively.[25] It was much used in the eighteenth century and beyond, alone or sometimes combined with rosewater. By the end of that century lemon zest or a bayleaf or cinnamon-stick are occasional alternatives, and the liqueurs ratafia or noyau are sometimes called for. Mrs Beeton remarked that 'a tablespoon of brandy, stirred in just before the blancmange is moulded, very much improves the flavour.'[26]

The earlier jellied blancmanges, set with hartshorn, needed the highly aromatic rosewater to help overcome the taste of the horn itself. Not surprisingly hartshorn fell out of favour with those who could afford better, and the recipes of the later eighteenth century are usually based on isinglasss, a purer form of gelatine, imported originally from Russia where it was obtained from sturgeons' heads. Isinglass even got a reputation as a health-food. Mrs Radcliffe in 1829 gave her recipe for an isinglass blancmange flavoured with orange-flower-water, and then continued: 'Blancmange … from its nourishing quality should never be absent from a genteel table, especially where any of the family or visitors have the smallest tendency to a decline. Indeed, though so great a delicacy, it may be considered as a most powerful medicine for consumptive habits.'[27]

In Victorian times hartshorn was replaced by commercially manu-factured gelatine, obtained from animal skins and bones, and less thoroughly purified than our gelatine today. Mrs Beeton preferred old-fashioned calf's foot jelly, but accepted that substitutes were very often used to 'lessen the expense and trouble…isinglass and gelatine being two of the principal materials employed. But', she added, 'although they may look as nicely as jellies made from good stock, they are never so delicate, having very often an unpleasant flavour, somewhat resembling glue, particularly when made from gelatine.'

Blancmange, like other jellied dishes of the day, was now usually set in elaborate fluted moulds, to be turned out onto a plate before it was brought to table. Mrs Beeton suggested the mould be oiled with 'purest salad oil' to ease turning out, and to give the blancmange 'a smooth, glossy appearance.'[28]

Another descendant of the medieval pottages with rice as thickener was rice cream, for which the ground rice was simmered with sugar, cream and rosewater. A plainer version, made with milk, was included among Robert May's blancmange recipes, and appeared in some eighteenth-century cookery books under the heading of rice blancmange. A different type of rice blancmange was made by soaking whole rice in water, then boiling it gently in milk, with sugar, and a little cinnamon and lemon-zest, until it became a mush, when it was put into a mould. When cold, it was solid enough to stand after it was turned out.

But in the early 1800s an alternative starch-based type emerged from the West Indies, when settlers began to exploit the processed roots of the arrowroot, a plant introduced there from Guiana. Soon arrowroot was being exported to Britain, and recipes appeared in England for its use in West Indian or American blancmange.[29] Meanwhile, the Americans themselves were experimenting with a new flour in the form of 'Oswego or Indian cornmeal', alias cornflour. It too travelled to England, where 'patent cornflour', was available as a commercial product by 1860. Two recipes for 'American blancmange' appeared in *Cassell's Dictionary of Cookery* about 1881, one based on arrowroot and the other on cornflour.

By then England's blancmange was itself on the way to becoming a commercial product. Its final manifestation came about after the invention of a substitute for egg custard. Alfred Bird's wife could not tolerate eggs, and in 1837 he devised for her a new form of custard based upon cornflour combined with milk, sugar, yellow colouring and vanilla flavouring. He then saw a commercial opportunity in the mixing of cornflour, flavouring and colouring to provide a custard powder for instant use in the kitchen, where the cook could add sugar and warm milk and quickly turn it into something resembling superficially a traditional egg custard. He launched Bird's custard powder in 1846, and its success was such that it has been on the market ever since (with minor improvements developed over time).

The custard powder was soon followed by commercial blancmange powders, made with a range of flavourings and colourings, not very successfully at first, to judge by the comment in *Cassell's Universal Cookery Book* of 1901. Under the separate heading 'Blancmange powders' is the entry:

These are to be had of various flavours and colours, and are very handy for the quick preparation of a sweet, especially for hot weather. The powders of a few years ago were very inferior for the most part to those now offered.

Directions for use always accompany the powders; but we may remark that, even when directed to blend the powder with boiling milk, we have generally found it a great improvement to give the whole a final stir over the fire, as it seems to give smoothness and a little more body…A richer dish can be had by using a little cream in place of some of the milk. The same remarks apply to custard powder. We give recipes for the preparation of both; but we know that it is cheaper to buy them.[30]

Home-made powder was prepared from sago flour, with colourings and flavourings, though rice flour and cornflour could be included. Modern commercial cornflour, despite its name, can also be based on starch sources other than maize or Indian corn. And thus blancmange, the white feasting-dish of the medieval aristocracy, dwindled into the plebeian version boiled up on a gas or electric cooker ring in the twentieth-century kitchen.

BLAUMANG OF FISSH

Nym a pond of ris, seth hem fort [until] hit berste, let hem kele: cast therto mylk of two pond of almandes / nym ye perch other ye loppistere or drie haddok, tese thereto, and boille hit / cast therto sugar & gif forth.

(Bodleian Library, 'two odd leaves in MS Laud 553', in T. Austin, *Two Fifteenth-Century Cookery-Books*, 1888, p. 114.)

TO MAKE BLOMANGE OF ISINGLASS

Boil one Ounce of Isinglass in a Quart of Water 'till its reduced to a Pint, then put in the Whites of four Eggs, with two Spoonfuls of Rice Water, to keep the Eggs from Poaching, and Sugar to your Taste, and run it thro' a Jelly Bag, then put to it two Ounces of sweet, and one Ounce of bitter Almonds, give them a Scald in your Jelly, and put them thro' a Hair Sieve, put it in a China Bowl, the next Day turn it out, and stick it all over with Almonds blanched and cut lengthways: Garnish with green Leaves or Flowers.

(E. Raffald, *The Experienced English Housekeeper*, 1769, p. 171.)

AMERICAN BLANCMANGE

Mix half a pint of cold water with two ounces of arrow-root, let it settle for fifteen minutes, pour off the water, and add as table-spoonful of laurel-water, and a little sugar; sweeten a quart of new milk, boil it with a little cinnamon, and half the peel of a lemon, pick out the cinnamon and lemon, and pour the boiling milk upon the arrow-root, stirring all the time. Put it into a mould, and turn it out the following day.

(Mrs Dalgairns, *The Practice of Cookery*, Edinburgh, 1829, p. 305.)

NOTES

1. M. Rodinson, 'Recherches sur les documents arabes relatifs à la cuisine', *Revue des études islamiques* 17 (1949), p. 139.

2. C.B. Hieatt & S. Butler, *Curye on Inglysch* (E.E.T.S., S.S. 8) 1985, 2. Diversa servicia, nos. 14, 33; 3. Utilis coquinario, nos. 27–9; 4. Forme of cury, nos. 38, 200. C.B. Hieatt, ed., *An Ordinance of Pottage* (London, Prospect, 1988), p. 158, no. 68.

3. Hieatt & Butler (n. 2), 1. Diversa cibaria, no. 1.

4. T. Scully, *The Art of Cookery in the Middle Ages* (Woodbridge, Boydell, 1995), pp. 208–10.

5. Maistre Chiquart, *Du fait de cuisine* [1420], ed. T. Scully, Vallesia (1985), p. 144.

6. T. Austin, ed., *Two Fifteenth-Century Cookery-Books* (E.E.T.S., O.S. 91), 1888, p. 31, no. 138; Hieatt & Butler (n. 2), 2. Diversa servicia, no. 34.

7. Hieatt & Butler (n. 2), 2. Diversa servicia, no. 41; 3. Utilis coquinario, no. 32; Austin (n. 6), p. 24, no. 100; p. 29, no. 126.

8. Platina, *De honesta voluptate*, ed. M.E. Milham (Tempe, Arizona, Medieval & Renaissance Texts & Studies, 1998), pp. 292–3.

9. *A Proper Newe Booke of Cokerye*, facsimile edition, ed. A. Ahmed (Cambridge, Corpus Christi College, 2002), p. 51.

10. *Good Huswife's Handmaid for the Kitchen*, 1597, transcribed and ed. S. Peachey (Bristol, 1992), pp. 21; 17.

11. T. Dawson, *The good huswifes Iewell* (London, 1596), p. 29.

12. *Elinor Fettiplace's Receipt Book*, ed. H. Spurling (London, Routledge, 1986), pp. 82–3.

13. R. May, *The Accomplisht Cook*, 2nd ed. (London, 1665), pp. 297–300.

14. *Grand cuisinier* (Rouen, 1620), f.35v; *L'Escole parfaite des officiers de bouche* (Paris, 1662), p. 420.

15. N. de Bonnefons, *Les delices de la campagne*, 2nd ed. (Amsterdam, 1661), p. 377; F. Sandford, *The history of the Coronation of …James II* (London, 1687), p. 110.

16. F.P. de La Varenne, *Le vray cuisinier* (Paris, 1682), p. 105; and his *Le cuisinier françois* (Rouen, 1686), p. 116.

17. *John Evelyn, Cook*, ed. C. Driver, (Blackawton, Prospect, 1997), p. 156, no. 290; P. Lamb, *Royal cookery* (London, 1710), pp. 125–7.

18. Austin (n. 6), p. 37, no. 17; T. Dawson, *The second part of The Good Huswives Iewell* (London, 1597), p. 19; J. Murrell, *Two Books of Cookerie and Carving, the fifth time printed with new additions* (London, 1638), pp. 81–2.

19. Murrell (n. 18), pp. 80–1.

20. May (n. 13), p. 204

21. R. Briggs, *The English Art of Cookery* (London, 1788), p. 456; J. Mollard, *The Art of Cookery* (London, 1801), p. 187; E. Raffald, *The Experienced English Housekeeper* (Manchester, 1769), p. 171.

22. M. Eales, *Receipts* (London, 1718), p. 84.

23. J. Bell, *A Treatise on Confectionery* (Newcastle, 1817), p. 63.

24. M.E. Rundell, *A New System of Domestic Cookery* (London, 1806), pp. 164–5.

25. R. Price, *The Compleat Cook*, ed. M. Masson (London, Routledge, 1974), p. 171; Evelyn (n. 17), p. 156.

26. I. Beeton, *The Book of Household Management* (London, 1861), p. 706.

27. M. Radcliffe, *A Modern System of Domestic Cookery* (London, 1829), p. 432.

28. Beeton (n. 26), pp. 709; 707.

29. Mrs Dalgairns, *The Practice of Cookery* (Edinburgh, 1829), p. 305; *Cassell's Domestic Dictionary* (London, c. 1884), under 'Blancmange'.

30. L. Heritage, *Cassell's Universal Cookery Book* (London, 1901), p. 945.

CHAPTER FIVE

FOREIGN OR ENGLISH?
A TALE OF TWO DISHES: OLIOS AND FRICASSEES

Gilly Lehmann

Following the development of a specific dish offers an opportunity to examine the changes it underwent, in cooking methods and flavourings, as it adapted to shifts in taste. In the case of olios and fricassees, there is also the question of the assimilation (or not) of a dish of foreign origin: did it become part of the national repertoire, and if so, when and how? Our two dishes offer parallels and contrasts. The history of the olio is a short one: the dish was one of the key items of late seventeenth-century court cookery, and although the olio is still found in many eighteenth-century cookery-books, it was past its heyday by 1750. Beyond this date, only the most ambitious or traditionalist books such as those by Martha Bradley or J. Skeat, still have receipts (hers taken from Vincent La Chapelle);[1] while mainstream works like the two best-sellers, Glasse (1747) and Raffald (1769), are silent on the subject. While flavourings changed, the olio was always recognizably the same dish, and this is the key to its demise: it was part of a grandiose and very masculine style of cookery, while in England, cookery was largely in the hands of women, and attempts to adapt the olio were not very successful. The fricassee, a more accessible dish for the woman cook, lasted for much longer, and is still a recognizable term today, but its early history is complicated by the uncertainty of its identity. Our first task is therefore to define the dishes and to examine the history of the terms, before embarking on an analysis of the origins and development of each dish and trying to link this to wider trends.

DEFINING THE 'OLIO', ITS ORIGINS AND ITS LIFESPAN

The 'olio' is defined by *OED* as 'a dish of Spanish and Portuguese origin, composed of pieces of meat and fowl, bacon, pumpkins, cabbage, turnips, and other ingredients stewed or boiled together and highly spiced; by extension, any dish containing a great variety of ingredients, a hotchpotch', with the first attestation in a culinary sense in 1643, in a letter by Sir John Suckling. Figurative meanings followed on rapidly, with the fairly derogatory idea of a medley appearing in 1648, and a collection of artistic or literary pieces in 1655. The term 'hotchpotch' had appeared earlier, in 1583, although it was itself a corrupted form of 'hotchpot' or 'hochepot', which had been current since the fifteenth century, although, as we shall see, this hardly corresponds to the definition above. The word followed the same line of development into figurative meaning as 'olio'.

In fact, the olio had appeared as a dish some time before this first attestation, but under a garbled form of its original Spanish name, *olla podrida*. (A literal translation gives the meaning 'rotten pot'; more loosely, 'mixed hotpot'.) The earliest printed receipt for the olio is found in an early seventeenth-century book, whose receipts originated in the Elizabethan period. Gervase Markham's *English Hus-wife* (1615) gives an 'Olepotrige', described as a 'principall dish of boild meate which is esteemed in all Spaine', and consisting of a huge variety of ingredients, meats and vegetables, cooked together in what amounts to a glorified *pot au feu*.[2] The more orthodox spelling soon took over as the dish became more popular. A transitional version of the name was used by Robert May in 1660: his book opens with an 'Olio Podrida', an enormously complex receipt using every imaginable meat, with a 'garnish' including marrow pies, and, for an 'extraordinary Olio', pies, salads, tarts and jellies as well.[3] But by now the Spanish term was more usually abbreviated to its first word; the spelling 'olio' was preferred by those books closest to French cookery, while others picked an Italianized orthography of the Spanish word. In 1655 *The Compleat Cook* gave 'A Spanish Olio', and those enthusiastic amateurs John Evelyn and Sir Kenelm Digby copied down receipts for an 'Oglio spanish', and 'A plain but good Spanish Oglia'.[4]

The Spanish origin of the dish is certain, and modern commentators suggest that it is a dish of great antiquity. The theory is that the name of the dish comes from the cooking pot, the *olla*, narrower at the top than at the bottom, which was being produced in the Iberian peninsula during the Bronze Age; the use of the term had been extended to the contents of the pot by the medieval period.[5] A further suggestion by Claudia Roden is that the dish has close links with the Jewish *adafina*, once a lamb stew with onions and chickpeas, left to cook overnight for the Sabbath, whose origins may be found in the Hispano-Arabic-Jewish cuisine of the thirteenth century, since the word apparently derives from the Arabic *al-dafinah*: the Arabic word means 'the buried treasure', and the Jewish stew-pot would be left buried under hot embers to cook. Today, there are resemblances between the modern Jewish *adafina* and the Spanish descendant of the *olla podrida*, the *cocido madrileño*, a stew with a variety of meats and including the chickpeas and saffron which were essential ingredients in most English seventeenth-century versions of the *olla*, but without the hard-boiled eggs which are typical of the *adafina*.[6]

Attractive though this theory is, there are serious weaknesses in the links, and it would perhaps be rash to see the olio in its seventeenth-century incarnation as originating in the medieval period. The thirteenth-century Arabic-Andalusian receipt for a 'Stuffed Buried Jewish Dish' mentioned by Roden is for spiced meatballs cooked between layers of spiced omelette; while the connexion with *adafina* seems clear, this is a long way from the *olla*. When the *olla* finally appears in Spanish cookery-books, it does not resemble the lamb stew which Roden quotes as being one of the clandestine dishes which led Jewish women to the stake under the Inquisition. There is no trace of the *olla* as a dish in the cookery book by Mestre Robert (alias Ruperto de Nola), known today as the *Libre del Coch*, which was probably written in the late fifteenth century by the cook to Ferdinand I of

Naples; it was printed in 1520 in Catalan, appeared in Castilian in 1525, and was reprinted until 1577. The book contains numerous references to the *olla* as the cooking pot in its receipts for *potajes* (these are receipts for the medieval stews and purées which were all considered as 'potages'), but the name does not seem to have been transferred to the dish itself.[7] The first printed Spanish receipt I have found dates from 1599, in Diego Granado's *Libro de cozina*. But the receipt was in fact part of the very extensive borrowings from Bartolomeo Scappi's *Opera*, published in Venice in 1570; Granado took 55 receipts from Nola and translated the rest of his material from Scappi. This version calls for the usual large quantities of different meats, plus vegetables including chickpeas, with a seasoning of pepper and cinnamon, but no saffron.[8] In other words, a variation of the dish we find in the English cookery books.

As the receipts noted earlier show, the olio was becoming a familiar dish in mid seventeenth-century England. The author of the *Compleat Cook*'s receipt professed himself 'utterly against those confused Olios, into which men put almost all kinds of meats and Roots',[9] a sign that the olio was well-known and often made, at least in pre-Civil War court circles. All the indications are that the dish and most of the receipts for it came directly from Spain. Evelyn obtained his receipt, probably in 1649, from the ambassador to Spain, Sir Arthur Hopton.[10] And twenty years later, Pepys ate an olio twice in 1669. On the first occasion on 5 April it was prepared by a cook who had been with Lord Sandwich in Spain, and Pepys commented that 'the Oleo was endeed a very noble dish'; a month later, on 5 May, he was able to compare this to the Spanish ambassador's version, but found the second inferior.[11]

All these references pre-date the appearance of the olio in French cookery-books: La Varenne (*Le Cuisinier françois*, 1651) has no receipt for an olio, neither does Pierre de Lune (*Le Cuisinier*, 1656), nor L.S.R. (*L'Art de bien traiter*, 1674). Intriguingly, John Evelyn's cookery manuscript contains a receipt for 'Pease pottage', a puréed soup poured over sops soaked in garlic-flavoured butter; the receipt concludes with the comment that 'this is the French olio, and excellent dish.'[12] La Varenne's book offers no such comment on his various *potages* based on pea purée, but the frequent use of salted goose (*oye*) or giblets (*la petite oye*) suggests a straight confusion here with *oil* or *oille*, as the later olio was known in France.[13] The adoption of the olio by the French as part of their court cookery came somewhat later. Two versions of the true *oil*, for flesh days and fasting days, appear in Massialot's *Cuisinier roïal et bourgeois* (1691), and the publication of the English translation of the book in 1702 was to extend the perception of the olio from simply a Spanish import to one of the most prestigious dishes of the court cooks' repertoire.[14] Whether in *The Court and Country Cook*, or in the books by the English court cooks, there is less emphasis on Spain: the court cooks were concerned with fashionable French cookery, and from their point of view, the olio was part of the series of *grosses entrées* which also included bisques and terrines. While court cookery reigned supreme, the dish was to be found in most of the more upmarket cookery-books, but with the advent of *nouvelle cuisine* in the 1730s it began to fall from favour, although the grand French books continued to supply receipts. Vincent La Chapelle gives several, but by the time the English translation of Menon's *Les Soupers de la Cour* (1755) came out in 1767, there was confusion between the olio and the terrine, a sign of waning prestige, even though the tendency was for the olio to become a vegetable soup.[15]

Meanwhile, most English books quietly abandoned these grandiose dishes, and the olios, bisks and terrines disappeared. Only the most exhaustive books continued to give receipts. Martha Bradley's two versions of the dish, described as 'the most pompous' made dishes, are for a French and a Spanish olio: the first is described as a 'plain French Olio', while the second is 'the true Spanish Olio', considered 'much better and richer than the French'. It is also more authentic, since, as Mrs Bradley points out, 'the Olioes were an Invention of the Spanish'. Incidentally, these comments do not appear in the original receipts which Mrs Bradley took from Vincent La Chapelle (although the titles of his receipts indicate that one of them is Spanish); they also mark a return to the origins of the dish, which was reverting to its earlier identity, before it had been taken up by French court cookery. Outside the cookery-books, one finds occasional references to the olio, even as late as 1785, when James Boswell records consuming one: 'Eat an olio with T.D.',[16] but the precise nature of the dish is impossible to determine, and the lack of comment again suggests that the olio no longer carried its former prestige.

Although Alan Davidson says that the term olio 'enjoyed wide currency in English in the 17th and 18th centuries, and indeed for much of the 19th century too',[17] receipts become increasingly thin on the ground.

Ude's book, *The French Cook* (1813) has no receipt, and in the English translation of Carême's work in 1836, olios are mentioned in the chapter on Spanish soups (but no receipts are given), simply to denounce La Chapelle's olio as 'repulsive'.[18] John Mollard has two olios, one Spanish, one English, but it is plain that the reader is not expected to use the Spanish receipt, since the author announces that 'this receipt for a spanish olio is only written to show how expensive a dish may be made', and he proposes an English substitute, which turns out to be oxtail soup.[19] Another English author who offers receipts, Richard Dolby, lifts two of them from Martha Bradley.[20] But by this date, most English authors had ceased to offer receipts for a dish which had long fallen out of fashion. Thus the olio had a fairly short lifespan, and it did not change much over the period, except in the nature of the flavourings which were added to the basic *pot au feu*.

CHANGING FLAVOURS AND THEIR SIGNIFICANCE

Markham's 'Olepotrige' is made of beef, mutton, pork, venison, veal, kid, lamb, sucking pig, pullet, partridge, chicken, quails, rails, blackbirds, larks, sparrows and other birds, all added progressively to the pot with various roots (potatoes, turnips, skirrets) and leaves; the broth is seasoned with sugar, spices (cloves, mace, cinnamon, ginger and nutmeg) and verjuice, and the solids are dished on sippets laid in chargers, covered with boiled dried fruit, then with the 'herbs', then with slices of orange and lemon, and finally a good sprinkling of sugar.[21] Not surprisingly, the cook is told that he will need a very large pot to cook all these items. What is not pointed out is that one would also need the services of a muscular cook to lift such a full pot on and off the fire. Two ingredients often considered obligatory for an olio, chickpeas and saffron, are conspicuously absent from Markham's version, which is typical of the Elizabethan preoccupation with the balance of sweet and sour elements. The very visible final garnish of citrus fruit and sugar is another typically sixteenth-century touch. The flavourings of this dish look very much older than those of the Spanish receipt from 1599 (or rather, from 1570), which uses cinnamon and pepper, but no sugar. Scappi and Granado's receipt is closer to later English versions than to Markham's, and his flavours show that England lagged behind Italian trends, although one might argue that Markham's receipt possibly dates back to the middle of the sixteenth century, given the warning to the reader on the reverse of his title-page that the receipts are not by him, but by 'an honorable Personage of this kingdome, who *was* singular amongst those of her ranke ...' (my italics).

Mid seventeenth-century olio receipts, which still consider the dish as Spanish, show the shifting trends in flavours. The most striking feature is the use of saffron and often optional garlic. *The Compleat Cook*'s version has these ingredients to flavour the broth from cooking beef, mutton, a hen and pigeons, plus the chickpeas which were part of the authentic Spanish dish. (While many English receipts specify chickpeas, some simply require peas instead, and this may have helped to create the confusion of nomenclature in Evelyn's manuscript.) The other spices were pepper and cloves, the herbs mint and parsley. The broth was to be served in porringers and drunk separately without sops, and the meat eaten with 'sauce' made of mustard and sugar. Digby's 'plain' version involves much the same meats (beef, mutton, veal, capon, pigeon), plus the usual vegetables including chickpeas, seasoned with cloves, nutmeg and saffron; garlic and 'sweet herbs' are optional. He recommends putting bread to soak in the pot, or, a very English touch, venison pie crust. John Evelyn's 'Spanish' version also contains saffron, and peas rather than chickpeas, but says that the beef is not usually served at grand feasts, although the other meats would have fed large numbers anyway. Not only are these far simpler dishes than Markham's, but the indiscriminate spicing and the sweet-and-sour elements in his broth and in the garnish have been eliminated.

The later court-cooks' olios tended to be more extravagant versions of Digby, and where the dish was still perceived as Spanish, the chickpeas (or sometimes peas) and saffron remained obligatory ingredients. Given its lavishness, the olio left plenty of scope for variations, and it is easy to see that each cook made his own. Massialot's version took the usual mix of butcher's meat, poultry and vegetables, and added spices (pepper, cloves, nutmeg, coriander-seed and ginger) plus thyme and basil to the broth; the meat was piled up on top of soaked bread, and the broth poured over. The instructions for serving show that diners were still expected to drink the broth first before proceeding to the solids.[22] In the hands of the English court cooks, the olio varied considerably, but what they all had in common was the way the dish was presented, with the meats piled up to form a pyramid. This presentation points to a change of emphasis, with the solids now more important than the broth, as is confirmed by Henry Howard's 'olea', where the broth becomes a claret-based sauce, thickened with eggs.[23] Patrick Lamb's receipt equals Markham's in its extravagance, but the flavours have of course changed to the purely savoury.[24] Charles Carter's is emphatically Spanish, in its title ('Olio Podreda, or Spanish Olio') and in its ingredients (chickpeas and saffron, amongst the welter of meats, vegetables, and additional garnishes); what has changed here is that most of the broth is apparently discarded, since the final pyramid of meats is covered with a raggoo garnish before being sent to table.[25] By the time one reaches Martha Bradley's receipts in 1756, the French olio is served in a tureen, with sops at the bottom of the dish, followed by the broth, with pieces of vegetables and choice pieces of the meats plus the pigeons whole; the Spanish version is dished up with the solids only, followed by the chickpeas in gravy and a little broth: the reader is reminded that 'it is not a Soup, but an Olio, the Things are to be eaten in Preference of the Liquor.' But the cook might send up basins of the broth, with toasted bread to accompany it, to satisfy old-fashioned tastes. The saffron has disappeared, even from the Spanish version, which is seasoned with basil and cloves, while the French olio has only herbs. Meanwhile in French cookery, the olio was turning into a vegetable soup, as noted earlier.

It is clear that the early eighteenth century saw the culmination of the olio as a fashionable dish, an important item in court coookery. But such an extravagant concoction was feasible only in the grandest kitchens. Cookery-books aimed at those below the level of the peerage had perforce to propose simplified versions, and the result was to take the dish a long way from its 'pot au feu' origins. The women's books of the late seventeenth century offered olios where separately-cooked ingredients were assembled in the serving dish to give the requisite presentation. Hannah Wolley's olio in 1670 involved starting with a 'Fricasy made of a Calves-head', and adding to this marrow-bones, boiled pigeons and a boiled salted goose, with a garnish of veal sweetbreads, sausage-meat balls, collops of veal or mutton, and in an echo of Markham, slices of orange and lemon with toasts for the marrow. All the items were cooked separately and assembled in the dish.[26] A similar version is found in Rebecca Price's manuscript receipt collection which was begun in 1681.[27] In the seventeenth century, one sometimes finds receipts for dishes where the term 'olio' is clearly used in the sense of a mix of lots of ingredients, as for instance in the 'olio pie' in the Martha Washington MS.[28] This may well be an early receipt, since the flavourings are a mix of sweet and savoury, while Wolley's and Price's receipts contain no sugar.

In spite of these signs of attempts at adaptation, the olio never became part of the English repertoire. It is not difficult to see why. Even where its Spanish associations lingered, the dish had become assimilated to French-inspired court cookery; it was baroque in its profusion of ingredients and in its pyramid presentation and was thus bound to fall quickly out of fashion. Furthermore, court cookery was an emphatically masculine preserve, while the much more English range of dishes was being maintained and developed by women cooks. With the fall from favour of court cookery in the 1730s amongst the fashionable followers of *nouvelle cuisine*, there was no longer any point in women cooks trying to produce more 'domestic' versions of the olio, which belonged to the earlier style. In fact, the chain of emulation was breaking; there was a rejection both of the 'disguised' food of the court style, and of the 'insubstantial' new style, and all that survived to give a modish air to more basic dishes was the raggoo-garnish which was an essential part of the court style. The olio pie had an equally short life: since English pies tended to include many ingredients in their fillings anyway, there was nothing peculiarly specific in the 'olio' name, and as the olio itself faded from the scene, so did its incarnation as a pie.

DEFINING THE 'FRICASSEE' AND ITS IDENTITY

The *OED* defines 'fricassee' as 'meat sliced and fried or stewed and served with sauce' or 'now usually a ragout of small animals or birds cut in pieces', and the first attested use of the term is in 1568 (in the revised edition of Sir Thomas North's translation of Guevara's *Diall of princes*); the second example quoted by *OED* is from Dawson's *The good huswifes Iewell*, part 2 (1586). The term is of course of French origin; the *TLF* (2002) dates the term to *c.* 1450, and defines it as cut-up meat, fish or vegetables cooked as a stew, while the *Nouveau Petit Robert* (1993) is more precise, defining a fricassée as pieces of poultry or white meat sautéed in butter and then stewed in sauce. The etymology of the word is supposed to be via the combination of two verbs, *frire* (fry) and *casser* (break). In modern English usage, most of us would probably follow Alan Davidson's remarks in *The Oxford Companion to Food* (1999) and substitute 'and' for 'or' in *OED*'s first definition. From these attestations it would appear that the fricassee entered the English culinary repertoire from France in the late sixteenth century, slightly earlier than the olio. The reality is rather more complex.

In fact, the dish as defined by *OED* was being made well before the name appeared, and when the name did appear, it was briefly applied to a very different type of dish, in a classic case of linguistic confusion. The fricassee was around long before the vocabulary caught up. The combination of two cooking methods, frying and simmering, points to a medieval origin, although the medieval method might reverse the order, and simmer first, before frying, in order to produce a contrast of textures, or might parboil or boil, then fry, then simmer. All of these combinations of cooking method produced a dish which in France was classified as a *potage*, the *potage* being what was poured over the solid ingredients before serving.[29] In other words, *potage* was a sauce rather than a soup. (In England, 'potage' was even more various, the term covering all sorts of dishes from venison with frumenty to jellies and fruit compôtes, but even here, the basic definition of some form of solids with a liquid or solidified sauce applies.) What we now consider as the fricassee technique appears in several medieval receipt collections, although it does not appear to be associated with any particular name of dish; another point is that such receipts are more numerous in fourteenth than in fifteenth-century collections. One finds the frying-and-simmering combination associated with 'bruets', 'hochepots', 'cyvees', and 'stewyde' dishes, but the association is never systematic.[30] The only type of dish which almost invariably calls for the technique is the 'egerdouce'.[31] What made the specificity of a dish at this period was the combination of ingredients, textures or flavours rather than the culinary technique.

Not until the sixteenth century do we begin to find dishes with a name which evokes the fricassee. A. W.'s *Book of Cookrye*, first published in 1584, contains three receipts for a 'fricace', surprisingly in the roast section of the book, with instructions to chop pre-cooked meat or fish which is then fried in butter and seasoned with ginger.[32] The second part of *The good huswifes Iewell* (1586) contains three receipts for 'fricasies': all are based on offal of some kind (lamb's head and 'purtenances' – heart, liver and lungs; neat's feet, or tripe), and the meat is always fried in butter but not simmered in a sauce. The first receipt bastes the meat with egg yolks before frying.[33] By 1615, Markham's *English Hus-wife* was giving similar receipts, in the first of the sections on cookery, devoted to 'Sallats and Fricases', with a definition: 'Fricases, or Quelque choses, [...] are dishes of manie compositions, and ingredients; as Flesh, Fish, Egges, Hearbes and many other things, all beeing prepared and made ready in a frying panne'.[34] Markham's 'simple fricases' are bacon and eggs, his 'compound fricases' include tansies, fritters and pancakes. Thus the name is now firmly attached to a cooking method, frying; and Markham's 'Quelque chose' (a variant 'fricase' with dried fruit and chopped pig's trotters mixed with eggs and cream and fried in butter), along with his other 'compound' dishes, is seen as an exotic import, 'beeing things of great request and estimation in Fraunce, Spaine, and Italy'. Later editions of *The English Hus-wife* which include instructions for feasts show that the 'fricases' and 'quelquechoses' were side dishes to fill up the gaps on the table.

This is a long way from the modern idea of a fricassee, and in fact the term 'fricase' as used here is a corruption of the 'fraise' or 'froise', a dish which can be found much earlier in English cookery-books. The late fourteenth-century *Diversa Servicia* gives a 'froys' (R18), consisting of cooked minced veal mixed with breadcrumbs, pepper and saffron, fried and then compressed to make a solid 'cake' for serving. In the fifteenth century, eggs were being added to the minced meat to bind the mixture, as in the 'froyse' receipts of Harleian MSS 279 (R lvii) and 4016, but this did not become universal. The 'Frasye at nyght' in *A Proper newe Booke of Cokerye* (1557/8) uses chicken giblets chopped and boiled, finished at the end with parsley, verjuice and a large amount of butter.[35] The versions from the 1580s are similarly close to the fourteenth-century dish. But at some point in the late sixteenth century eggs came to be the dominant ingredient, as in Markham's receipts. Another late sixteenth-century version was Elinor Fettiplace's 'light frayse', a cross between an omelette and a pancake.[36] There seems to be considerable overlap here, with some of the printed receipts for 'fricases' close to the fourteenth-century 'froyse', others closer to the later version with eggs. What is puzzling is why Markham should see his 'compound fricases' as foreign, when such egg and chopped meat mixtures had been around for at least a century and a half. One notes also that it is in fact the fraize which was seen as fashionably foreign, and not the fricassee as we understand it. And the reference is to Spain and Italy as well as to France, allegedly the source of the word 'fricassee' and of the dish.

The confusion between the fricassee and the fraize persisted well into the seventeenth century. Both were prepared in a frying-pan, and early definitions of the fricassee are sufficiently vague to cover both dishes. Thus Cotgrave's dictionary of 1611 defines a 'fricassée' as 'any meat fried in a panne'. At the beginning of the century, receipts labelled 'fricassee' are usually for fraizes: John Murrell's *New Booke of Cookerie* (1615) has a 'Fregesy of Egges' in the puddings section; here a batter of cream, eggs, sugar and spice is fried in two layers, with fried apples in between.[37] One can see how the term gradually shifted towards its modern meaning: when the English translation of La Varenne's book came out in 1653, the glossary defined a 'Fricasseé [sic]' by saying 'It is a frying with a sauce.'[38] This is still not necessarily the modern fricassee, however, since stewing is not specified. In the 1650s, fricassees and fraizes are found together: Jos. Cooper's 'Frikese' (i.e. fricassee) receipts are grouped with receipts for frying which cover a wide range of dishes, from fricassees to fritters.[39] A little later, William Rabisha's section (Book X) on 'Frigasies and Frying' also shows this confusion: the common element in all his receipts is frying, but the fricassees (meat fried and then served with a sauce thickened with egg yolks) appear alongside an 'amlett', a 'phraise', tansies and pancakes.[40] Significantly, Robert May's *Accomplisht Cook* (1660) has a true fricassee, called 'A rare Fricase', amongst the boiled meats; at last the fricassee is recognized as belonging to stewing rather than frying. But May gives two other receipts similar to Murrell's, and more generally still uses the old terms in his receipts for a 'Quelque shose [sic]' and a 'Fricase' – the terms are clearly interchangeable – all prepared like the omelettes which also appear in this section of the book on eggs. But there are signs that the vocabulary was changing, and that the use of the word 'Fricase' to refer to a fraize was on the way out: the receipts mention cooking the eggs as 'omlets' or as a 'tansie'.[41] Thus by the 1660s the confusion of terms was beginning to be resolved, and the terms 'omelette' and 'fraize' would soon oust 'fricase' when it came to egg dishes, although their meanings became more specific, with the fraize coming to designate a dish made by frying a batter of egg and other ingredients: Hannah Glasse gives two receipts, one for 'apple frazes' which are like fritters but shallow rather than deep-fried, and an 'almond fraze', a kind of solid almond custard made like an omelette.[42]

After this excursion into fraizes, we must return to the fricassee. In the late sixteenth-century cookery-books, there were a few receipts for more recognizable fricassees, albeit without the name. Dawson's receipt 'To frie Chickins' follows the medieval practice of cooking the chickens in broth first, then jointing them, frying them in butter and finishing the dish by stewing them briefly in a sauce made of broth and verjuice, seasoned with nutmeg, cinnamon, ginger and pepper, and with an egg-yolk liaison to finish.[43] A notable feature here is the absence of sugar, still a frequent ingredient in receipts at this period (Dawson's two parts use sugar in 64 per cent and 48 per cent of the receipts). It must be noted, however, that such receipts for what we would consider as fricassees are rare: most of the stewed meats in these late sixteenth-century books are simply simmered in liquid, and served with sops to absorb some of the sauce if necessary. A further point is that the dish was developing before the modern name became attached to it. Even in 1655, *The Compleat Cook*'s most 'modern' fricassee is entitled 'To fry Chickens'.[44] So it seems that the use of the French word was a linguistic rather than a culinary borrowing.

The gap between the vocabulary and the dish was not closed until the second half of the seventeenth century. This is seen first in manuscript receipts. The manuscript known as Martha Washington's contains two receipts for chicken-based fricassees, with the name spelt 'frykecy' or 'frykasy'.[45] Both call for pieces of meat to be fried in butter, but the first receipt then stews the meat with water, onion and herbs and finishes the dish with an egg-yolk liaison plus vinegar or lemon juice, while the second fries the meat until it is done, and finishes with a similar sauce, this time with spices as well as herbs. The MS copy written for William Penn Jr, of the receipts belonging to his mother, Gulielma Penn (1644–94), also has a 'Fregasy of Chicken', with the same type of sharp egg-thickened sauce.[46] It is difficult to put a date on these receipts, but the absence of sugar, and the changed spices (clove, mace, nutmeg and pepper in one, nutmeg in another) point to the mid seventeenth century. The egg-yolk liaison, just as in Dawson's receipt, suggests a link with the fraize, and perhaps a further explanation for the confusion of terms: frying-pans and eggs were involved in both dishes. What we know as a fricassee was beginning to emerge: meat, usually chicken, fried and then stewed in a sauce which was thickened at the end of the cooking time.

THE FLAVOURS AND TECHNIQUES OF THE FRICASSEE

By the middle of the seventeenth century, today's fricassee was beginning to emerge from the linguistic and culinary confusion, but as is so often the case, printed books lagged behind, offering a mix of old and new flavourings, and varied culinary methods. These mixes of old and new are found in the cookery-books of the 1650s and 1660s. In 1654 *The Ladies Cabinet Enlarged and Opened* gives four 'Frigasie' receipts (these receipts do not appear in the 1639 edition). In three of them, slices of lamb, rabbit or veal are fried and then finished with an egg and verjuice sauce; in the chicken fricassee the meat is 'fried' in water and butter, the cooking liquid being finished with sugar and verjuice.[47] Jos. Cooper's receipts for a 'Frikese', published in the same year, offer the modern method, but some old-fashioned flavours, with sauces which are acid and very heavily buttered, with sugar in two of the four receipts, and in one of these two, dates.[48] The sweet-acid combination, and the heavy buttering, are all characteristic of the early seventeenth century and even before. After the fricassees come receipts to 'fry' various fish and vegetables: some of these receipts are for fricassees, such as the turbot. Thus although the term 'frikese' is now firmly attached to the fricassee, one also continues to find the dish without its new name. Rabisha's eight 'Frigacy' receipts mix the newer anchovy-wine (3 receipts) or herb-wine (3 receipts) flavouring, and the older sugar-acid combination (2 receipts). Robert May's only 'true' fricassee, using pigeons and chickens, is unusual for its elaborate court-style garnish involving lamb-stones, sweetbreads, asparagus, marrow, oysters, pistachios and almonds, all bathed in an egg and verjuice sauce.[49] Gradually, the sauces with sugar, and more slowly those with verjuice, were being eliminated.

The Compleat Cook (1655) offers further evidence for the gradual development of new flavours, while at the same time showing the lingering confusion between the fricassee and the fraize. A group of three receipts 'to fricate' things, two for offal and one for mushrooms, uses similar methods: the meats are 'fried' in broth and butter, the mushrooms stewed in their own juices then fried in butter, and all are finished by 'tossing' with a savoury 'lear' of mutton gravy, citrus juice, egg yolks and nutmeg.[50] The stewing in sauce is not yet a feature of the method. Even closer to earlier practice is the receipt to 'fricate Beef Pallats', which are pre-cooked, seasoned and breadcrumbed, and then fried in butter ('so fricate them till they be brown on both sides') before being served with a sauce of mutton gravy, anchovy, nutmeg and lemon juice.[51] This is still very similar to the fourteenth-century 'froyse', but the sauce is far more modern. The treatment of chicken offers two illustrations of the way the dish was developing: 'To make a Fricake [sic]' is remarkably close to Dawson's receipt, with the meat stewed first in broth, then fried in butter, and finished with a sauce of verjuice, nutmeg and egg-yolks. The medieval cooking method lingers, the main change being the reduction in spices. 'To fry Chickens' is the most 'modern', since the chickens are browned in butter and then stewed between two dishes in mutton gravy, butter, onion, anchovy, nutmeg and salt.[52] The common denominator in this book is the use of mutton gravy and nutmeg.

The development of the fricassee as we know it coincides with the mid-seventeenth-century shift in flavours, away from the spiced and often sweetened sauces, and towards more savoury combinations, often involving meat juices or the anchovy-wine mix. The separation of sweet and savoury is usually attributed to French influence in the wake of the publication of La Varenne's *Cuisinier françois* in 1651, but the peculiarly English flavour associations of the newly savoury dishes found in ladies' manuscript receipts suggest that while French fashions assisted the movement, the underlying trend was already present in England. By the last decades of the seventeenth century, the brown and white fricassees which are standard items in eighteenth-century cookery-books had begun to appear in these collections. Rebecca Price has several fricassee receipts, using chicken, veal, rabbit, calves' liver, and one 'French Frikesy of pigions'.[53] The implication is of course that the other fricassees are not French. The cooking methods are very variable: frying followed by stewing; simply frying with a final saucing; simmering in water or broth; reheating slices of cold roast meat with a sauce, a technique more usually described as a 'hash'. As the 'French' receipt says, the meat could be 'fried' in water, the use of the frying-pan justifying the expression. The finished sauces are of two types: the older egg-yolk liaison, often with butter and verjuice added; and the new egg-yolk and cream to finish, for fricassees that are sometimes described as 'white'. Diana Astry's slightly later MS, dating from the first decade of the eighteenth century, gives a 'white frigcacee of chicken' with a cream sauce flavoured with onion, bacon, parsley, nutmeg, and a very modest quantity of vinegar. The instruction to 'cut them as usually do [sic] for a frigcacee' again points to the fact that this was a familiar dish. The receipt which follows for rabbits (or chicken) is for the other type, without cream, flavoured with the anchovy and wine combination which is characteristic of the late seventeenth century.[54] These are early examples of receipts which appear in most eighteenth-century books.

It is noticeable that seventeenth-century printed books and manuscript collections all give receipts for chicken, with lamb, veal, rabbit, or even hare as alternatives. The predominance of chicken was to continue as one moves towards the eighteenth century. Brown and white fricassees, the receipts invariably presented together, usually call for chicken or rabbit meat; Hannah Glasse offers the two, but is unusual in also suggesting brown and white fricassees of fish, using sole, skate or thornback.[55]

These paired receipts are found in the court cooks' books and in those aimed at a more modest readership. What differentiates the two types is the lavish garnishes of the court cooks' receipts (Charles Carter adds the usual truffles, morels, mushrooms, artichoke bottoms and sweetbreads to his white and brown fricassees[56]), and the persistence of the older flavourings in the domestic type of receipts. Edward Kidder's books of *c.* 1720 supply fairly standard versions of the latter, which were taken up later by E. Smith. The flavours are those of the manuscript receipts, anchovy and wine for the brown version, broth, cream and mushrooms for the white version. What is new here is the flour thickening, a brown roux for one, the 'bitt of butter rould up in flower' for the other.[57] (The flour thickening began as a stabilizer for the egg-yolk liaison and later replaced it.)

Variations on the theme developed: soon there were brown and white versions of 'Scotch collops', another standard dish made with slices of veal which had originated at about the same time;[58] by the 1740s there were also similar fricassees of eggs,[59] and other items joined this repertoire, such as sweetbreads.[60] Ann Cook proposes further variations on the colour theme, with her fricassees of chicken which may be yellow (with saffron), red (with lobster berries), and green (with asparagus, sorrel and parsley).[61] All these variations show how much the fricassee had become part of English cookery by the eighteenth century: Glasse has 22 fricassee receipts, for meat, but also for fish, eggs and vegetables; 12 of the 22 have cream sauces. Raffald, who places more emphasis on the dessert, has 10 fricassees, with 5 cream sauces. Even the cheaper cookery-books contain receipts for fricassees: Elizabeth Price's *New Book of Cookery* (c. 1780) gives 12.[62] In contrast, William Verral's cookery-book, based on his experience under that celebrated French cook, Pierre Clouet, gives only 6 (for eels in champagne, calves' tongues, chickens with mushrooms, tench with whiting livers, eggs 'a la tripe', and mushrooms[63]), and not the usual fricassees of the English books. Thus the English-style fricassees lived on, unaffected by the development of 'nouvelle cuisine', long after the demise of court cookery, contrary to the olio.

The frequency of these receipts, all with minor variations in the flavouring, is one sign of the assimilation of the dish. Obviously, the frequent borrowings between authors is a factor here, but the variations between receipts should perhaps be seen as a sign of familiarity rather than plagiarism. Another sign of assimilation is the 'codification' of fricassees. As we have seen, seventeenth-century receipts hesitated between cooking techniques and flavour combinations. What is striking in the eighteenth century is the stability of the basic receipts, which extends to what could be fricasseed: chicken and rabbit, pigeons; various items of offal, especially tripe, tongues and palates, and sweetbreads; vegetables such as mushrooms and artichoke bottoms; hard-boiled eggs. These are the basics one finds again and again. Brown fricassees required gravy and often wine, thickened with a roux or beurre manié; the egg-yolk liaison still added in some of Glasse's receipts soon disappeared. White fricassees took cream and egg-yolks, usually with beurre manié to stabilize the sauce, although it is noticeable that Raffald sees the flour as the main thickener, the earliest sign of the debasement to come. But these receipts did not, in fact, change much once they had appeared after the Restoration. English cookery also developed further variations on the theme which no longer mentioned the word 'fricassee' in the receipt title: 'Scotch collops' clearly belong to the genre, and later, curry could also be placed here (Charlotte Mason's receipt for curry begins, 'Cut two chickens as for a fricasee'[64]).

The examples cited above, dating from the Restoration onwards, show that the fricassee became part of the repertoire of English cooks, and more specifically of English women cooks. It was a dish which lent itself to small quantities, and although court cooks such as Charles Carter added a lavish garnish to the basic dish, this was simply an optional extra, unlike the huge variety of meats and vegetables which were essential to the olio.

The characteristic flavours of the English fricassee, the anchovy-wine combination and the cream sauce, are found first in ladies' manuscript cookery collections before they appear in print. Furthermore, receipts for the dish continued to appear well into the nineteenth century, especially in books by women: Mrs Rundell gives 9 receipts, Elizabeth Alcock 11, M. Radcliffe 9, whereas John Mollard has only 3, and Richard Dolby 5; Ude has one master-receipt for chicken, followed by variations.[65] Only in the 1840s does the fricassee begin to decline: Eliza Acton has only one receipt for chicken fricassee and, ominously, a fricassee sauce using 'common English white sauce'.[66] But until the 1830s, receipts still follow the style of their eighteenth-century predecessors, and belong to the domestic style of women's cookery. In spite of its name, the fricassee was more English than French.

In eighteenth-century cookery-books, fricassees are usually to be found in the chapters on 'made dishes', which were seen as the most fashionable ones. Although originally they may have been considered fashionable because of the French name, fricassees had become so familiar as to occasion no xenophobic outpourings. They did, however, belong to the realm of aspirational cookery. When in June 1757 Elizabeth Raper returned from a visit at one o'clock to find unexpected guests, she set to and made a fricassee and 'produced' herself in the parlour by two, although dinner was not served until three; her receipt book contains several fricassees.[67] In 1766 the Rev. John Penrose, taking the waters at Bath (he suffered from gout), was invited to dinner by his fellow-Cornishman Sir Booth Williams, and was given ' Scotch-Collops' and a 'Fricasee of Rabbits' at the first course;[68] in his lodgings with his family he ate humbler fare. Similarly, the Rev. James Woodforde's diary for the 1780s records several fricassees (of rabbit, fowl, and sweetbreads), but these were always eaten when he dined with the local squire; he does not seem ever to have served them himself. Here, the fricassee was a second-course dish, as for instance on 8 April 1783, when the dinner for seven people consisted of 'first Course – Fish, a Piece of rosted Beef, Mutton Stakes, Pork Stakes, Peas Soup, Potatoes baked, and a Yorkshire Pudding – 2nd Course – Fricasied Fowl, a rosted Pigg, Jellies, Tartlets, Lobster, Pickled Salmon, and Cheese-Cakes.'[69] The fricassee was a dish you invited a man to, not one for every day.

There is clear evidence of assimilation here too: the fricassee was food for entertaining, but its appearance occasioned no particular comment. Fricassees, like hashes, were the great survivors from the new style of cooking which had come in after the Restoration. In contrast to the olio, the fricassee was a simple dish to execute, well within the reach of the gentry kitchens where a woman cook presided, and it was a dish which lent itself to advance preparation, so that a lady could prepare it for serving later. It is easy to understand why such a dish should remain so popular. And yet these great eighteenth-century favourites became debased in the middle of the nineteenth century by becoming repositories for leftovers. The hash, usually made with partly-roasted meat in the seventeenth century, gradually changed into being made with cold meat. Hashes were often served at supper, and this was a useful way of creating a hot dish from the relics of dinner. The fricassee followed the same pattern, but rather later. By the time one reaches Mrs Beeton, the fricassee in the modern sense has become restricted to fowl, and is all too often considered as 'cold meat cookery' (2 of the 3 receipts are for leftovers[70]). Other receipts are either closer to the fraize, such as the 'fricasseed calf's feet', in which the feet are boiled, the meat then removed, cut up, battered and fried; or to hashes, such as the 'fricasseed calf's head', which again requires the remains of a boiled head, chopped and reheated in sauce. The fricassees slipped out of sight, and when Florence White edited her collection of traditional receipts, *Good Things in England*, in 1932, there was no sign of any such dish, although White listed Martha Bradley and Elizabeth Raffald amongst her sources. The white and brown fricassees, which had been part of English cookery for 150 years, were once again perceived as foreign.

With such an honourable history, it is time to revive the basic English brown and white fricassees, and for those prepared to launch into this project, I offer the following, which are Kidder's receipts as printed in the 1736 edition of E. Smith's *Compleat Housewife*. That quantities should be vague is no obstacle; remember that discretion is required for the anchovy component, which should add flavour without being perceptible as such. My personal variation mixes the two receipts, with anchovy, thyme, nutmeg and lemon peel to flavour the chicken stewed in white wine and broth, with mushrooms and a cream sauce to finish: be lavish with the cream and sparing with the flour, following the instructions to the letter!

A BROWN FRICASEE OF CHICKENS OR RABBITS.

Cut them in pieces, and fry them in butter; then having ready hot a pint of gravy, a little claret, white wine, strong broth, two anchovies, two shiver'd palates, a faggot of sweet herbs, savoury balls and spice, thicken it with brown butter, and squeeze on it a lemon.

A WHITE FRICASEE OF THE SAME.

Cut them in pieces, wash them from the blood, and fry them on a slow fire; then put them in a tossing pan, with a little strong broth; season them, and toss them up with mushrooms, and oysters; when almost enough, put to them a pint of cream, thicken it with a bit of butter rolled up in flour.

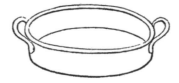

NOTES

1. See Martha Bradley, *The British Housewife* (1756; facs. repr. Totnes: Prospect, 1996–98), vol. 3, pp. 342–5; J. Skeat, *The Art of Cookery and Pastery* (London, 1769), pp. 17–18.

2. [Gervase Markham], *The English Hus-wife* (London, 1615), pp. 49–50.

3. May, *The Accomplisht Cook* (1660; facs. repr. of 1685 edition, Totnes: Prospect, 1994), pp. 1–5.

4. W. M., *The Compleat Cook* (1655; facs. repr. of 1671 edition, London: Prospect, 1984), pp. 92–3; Christopher Driver (ed.), *John Evelyn, Cook* (Totnes: Prospect, 1997), pp. 75–6; Digby, *The Closet [...] Opened* (1669; repr. ed. Jane Stevenson & Peter Davidson, Totnes: Prospect, 1997), p. 137.

5. Alicia Rios & Lourdes March, *The Heritage of Spanish Cooking* (London: Ebury, 1992), p. 50.

6. For a discussion of these links, see Claudia Roden, *The Book of Jewish Food* (London: Viking, 1997), pp. 189, 191, 192, 367; see also Rafael Chabrán, 'Medieval Spain', in Melitta Weiss Adamson (ed.), *Regional Cuisines of Medieval Europe: A Book of Essays* (London: Routledge, 2002), p. 137. Rios & March give a receipt for the 'cocido madrileño', p. 60, but none for 'olla podrida'.

7. I consulted the second Castilian edition of this book: Ruperto de Nola, *Libro de Guisados* (Logroño: Miguel de Eguia, 1529; repr. ed. Dionisio Pérez, Madrid, 1929). Jeanne Allard's analysis of this book shows that although the translation added a few receipts, the basis of the book remained medieval; in later editions, more receipts were added, but the 'olla' was not amongst them. See Allard, 'Nola: rupture ou continuité?' in Carole Lambert (ed.), *Du manuscrit à la table* (Paris: Champion-Slatkine/Montreal: Presses de l'Université de Montréal, 1992), pp. 149–161.

8. Diego Granado, *Libro del Arte de Cocina* (Madrid: Luis Sanchez, 1599; repr. ed. Joaquín del Val, Madrid: Sociedad de Bibliófilos Españoles, 1971), pp. 75–6. For Granado's borrowings, see Allard's essay, p. 149. Allard gives the title of Granado's work as *Libro de cozina*, and the author's name as Diego Granado Maldonado. The book was reprinted in 1609 and in 1614.

9. W. M., *The Compleat Cook*, pp. 92–3.

10. See Driver (ed.), *John Evelyn, Cook*, pp. 75–6.

11. See Pepys, *Diary*, ed. Robert Latham & W. J. Matthews (London: Bell & Hyman, 1970–83), vol. 9, pp. 509, 544.

12. Driver (ed.), *John Evelyn, Cook*, pp. 45–6.

13. For La Varenne's pea soup receipts, see *Le Cuisinier françois* (1651; repr. of the Bibliothèque bleue edition, ed. Jean-Louis Flandrin, Philip & Mary Hyman, Paris: Montalba, 1983), pp. 122–3.

14. For the receipts, see [Massialot], *Le Cuisinier roïal et bourgeois* (1691; Paris: 1698), p. 336 ff; *The Court and Country Cook* (London, 1702), part 1, p. 166 ff.

15. See La Chapelle, *The Modern Cook* (London, 1733), vol. 1, pp. 2–5; B. Clermont, *The Professed Cook* (London, 1769), vol. 1, pp. 13, 29.

16. Irma S. Lustig & Frederick A. Pottle (eds), *Boswell: The Applause of the Jury, 1782–1785* (The Yale Edition of the Private Papers of James Boswell, vol. 11, London, 1982), p. 326.

17. Davidson, *The Oxford Companion to Food* (Oxford: Oxford UP, 1999), sub Olio.

18. [Antonin] Carême, *French Cookery*, tr. William Hall (London, 1836), pp. 56–59.

19. Mollard, *The Art of Cookery Made Easy and Refined* (London, 1801), pp. 32–38.

20. See Dolby, *The Cook's Dictionary, and House-keeper's Directory* (London, 1830), pp. 354–5.

21. Markham, *The English Hus-wife*, pp. 49–50.

22. [Massialot], *The Court and Country Cook*, part 1, pp. 166–7.

23. See Henry Howard, *England's Newest Way* (London, 1708), pp. 38–9.

24. See Lamb, *Royal Cookery* (London, 1710), pp. 30–35. Other court cooks' receipts for the

olio are found in R. Smith, *Court Cookery* (London, 1723), part 1, pp. 87–88; John Nott, *The Cook's and Confectioner's Dictionary* (London, 1723), O 31, O 32.

25. See Carter, *The Complete Practical Cook* (1730; facs. repr. London: Prospect, 1984), pp. 3–4.

26. Hannah Wolley, *The Queen-like Closet* (London, 1670), p. 197.

27. See Madeleine Masson (ed.), *The Compleat Cook* (London: Routledge, 1974), p. 90.

28. See Karen Hess (ed.), *Martha Washington's Booke of Cookery* (New York: Columbia UP, 1981), pp. 84–5.

29. For an analysis of 'potage' in the medieval period, see Françoise Sabban, 'Le savoir-cuire ou l'art des potages dans Le Ménagier de Paris et le Viandier de Taillevent', in *Manger et boire au Moyen Age: Actes du colloque de Nice* (1984), vol. 2, pp. 161–172.

30. Examples from the MSS edited by C. B. Hieatt & S. Butler, *Curye on Inglysch* (EETS SS 8, 1985) are the 'bruet of sarcynesse' (R55 in 'Diversa Servicia') and probably the 'bruet de Almayne' (R15 in 'Diversa Cibaria'); the 'gees in hochepot' (R22 in 'Diversa Servicia'); the 'plays in cyvee' and the 'tenches in cyuee' (R115 and 123 in the 'Forme of Cury'). Later MSS, such as the two fifteenth-century collections edited by Thomas Austin, *Two Fifteenth-Century Cookery-Books* (EETS OS 91, 1888, repr. 2000) give a receipt for stewing small birds (R.xix in Harleian MS 279). But other examples of these dishes do not call for a preliminary frying. The fact that the fourteenth-century collections contain more receipts, and that the slightly later Yale MS Beinecke 163 edited by C. B. Hieatt as *An Ordinance of Pottage* (London: Prospect, 1988) has no receipts using the fricassee technique, points to this type of method falling out of favour in the fifteenth century.

31. Examples are: 'Diversa Servicia' R60, 'Utilis Coquinario' R17, 'Forme of Cury' R137, all for fish, although in the last two the sauce is apparently simply poured over the fried fish, while the earlier receipt stews the fish in the sauce. 'Forme of Cury' also gives a meat-based 'Egurdouce' (R23) which does indicate frying followed by simmering. The 'Egredouncye' in Harleian MS 279 (R.cxl) calls for broiling the meat first rather than frying it.

32. A.W., *A Book of Cookrye* (London, 1591), f. 26.

33. ?Thomas Dawson, *The Second Part of the good Hus-wives Jewell* (London, 1597), pp. 11–12.

34. Markham, *The English Hus-wife*, pp. 42–3. The receipts are pp. 43–47.

35. See Anne Ahmed (ed.), *A Proper Newe Booke of Cokerye* (1557/8; facs. repr., Cambridge: Corpus Christi College, 2002), p. 74.

36. See Hilary Spurling (ed.), *Elinor Fettiplace's Receipt Book* (London: Viking Salamander, 1986), p. 174.

37. Murrell, *A New Booke of Cookerie* (1615; facs. repr. Amsterdam: Theatrum Orbis Terrarum, 1972), p. 36 (numbered 39 in the book).

38. [La Varenne], *The French Cook* (London, 1653), in the table of hard words.

39. See Jos. Cooper, *The Art of Cookery Refin'd and Augmented* (London, 1654), pp. 66–87.

40. See Rabisha, *The whole Body of Cookery Dissected* (1661; facs. repr. of 1682 edition, Totnes: Prospect, 2003), pp. 163–178.

41. May, *The Accomplisht Cook*, pp. 67, 446–7.

42. See Glasse, *The Art of Cookery, Made Plain and Easy* (1747; facs. repr. London: Prospect, 1983), p. 82.

43. See Dawson, *The good huswifes Iewell* (London, 1596), f. 25.

44. W. M., *The Compleat Cook*, p. 71.

45. Hess (ed.), *Martha Washington's Booke of Cookery*, pp. 40–44.

46. See Evelyn Abraham Benson (ed.), *Penn Family Recipes* (York, Pennsylvania: George Shumway, 1966), p. 29.

47. See Lord Ruthven, *The Ladies Cabinet Enlarged and Opened* (London, 1654), pp. 199–200.

48. See Cooper, *The Art of Cookery Refin'd and Augmented*, pp. 67–72.

49. See May, *The Accomplisht Cook*, p. 67.

50. See W. M., *The Compleat Cook*, pp. 7–9.

51. Ibid., p. 91.
52. Ibid., pp. 97, 71.
53. See Masson (ed.), *The Compleat Cook*, pp. 92–96.
54. See Bette Stitt (ed.), 'Diana Astry's Recipe Book', *Publications of the Bedfordshire Historical Record Society* 37 (1957), receipts 19 and 20, p. 93.
55. See Glasse, *The Art of Cookery*, pp. 14, 93–4.
56. See Carter, *The Complete Practical Cook*, pp. 74–5.
57. Kidder, *Receipts of Pastry and Cookery*, ed. David E. Schoonover (Iowa City: Iowa UP, 1993), p. 143; the receipts also appear in the printed versions of Kidder's book. The manuscript version also adds anchovy to the cream sauce, while the printed book does not. Kidder's receipts appear in the 7th edition of E. Smith's *The Compleat Housewife* (London, 1736) p. 35, but not in the original edition of 1727. The later edition took a total of 34 receipts from the printed version of Kidder's book.
58. To quote only two examples, Scotch collops appear in Glasse, *The Art of Cookery*, p. 13; brown and white versions in Elizabeth Raffald, *The Experienced English House-keeper* (1769; repr. Lewes: Southover, 1997), p. 49. Earlier examples are found in Cooper, *The Art of Cookery* (1654), p. 85; Hannah Wolley, *The Cooks Guide* (London, 1664), pp. 66–7; Digby, *The Closet Opened* (1669), pp. 139–40, 151–2; also in ladies' MSS: see Hess, p. 45, Masson, pp. 96–7; also among Elizabeth Freke's MS receipts, mostly copied out between 1684 and 1699: British Library, Add. MS 45718, f. 10. The earliest receipts often suggest slices of mutton, beef or veal, but by the end of the 17th century, veal has become the standard ingredient.
59. See, for instance, Elizabeth Moxon, *English Housewifry* (Leeds, [1741]), p. 40.
60. See Elizabeth Raffald, *The Experienced English House-keeper* (1769; repr. Lewes: Southover, 1997), pp. 50–51.
61. Ann Cook, *Professed Cookery* (Newcastle, 1754), pp. 73–4.
62. See Glasse, pp. 14–15, 23, 87, 90, 93–4, 97, 98, 101, 123; Raffald, pp. 50–51, 57, 61–2, 63, 67, 70–71, 143, 147; Price, in the section on made dishes, pp. 54–87.
63. William Verral, *A Complete System of Cookery* (1759; repr. as *William Verrall's Cookery Book*, ed. Ann Haly, Lewes: Southover, 1988), pp. 62, 86, 93, 96–7, 111, 117.
64. [Charlotte Mason], *The Lady's Assistant* (London, 1773), p. 245.
65. See [Maria Rundell], *A New System of Domestic Cookery* (London, 1810), pp. 39, 53, 63–4, 78–9, 84–5, 112–3, 172, 175; Alcock, *The Frugal Housekeeper's Companion* (Liverpool, 1812), pp. 42, 80, 92, 93–4, 96, 104–5, 188, 189, 205, 207; Radcliffe, *A Modern System of Domestic Cookery* (Manchester, 1823), pp. 59, 88, 113–4, 147–8, 189, 203, 225–6; Mollard, op. cit., pp. 117, 120, 167; Dolby, op. cit., pp. 153–4, 254, 429; Ude, op. cit., pp. 218–222.
66. Acton, *Modern Cookery, in all its Branches* (London, 1845), pp. 318–9, 122.
67. See Bartle Grant (ed.), *The Receipt Book of Elizabeth Raper* (Soho: Nonesuch, 1924), p. 14; for receipts, see pp. 55, 59, 62.
68. Brigitte Mitchell & Hubert Penrose (eds.), *Letters from Bath 1766–1767 by the Rev. John Penrose* (Gloucester: Alan Sutton, 1983), p. 127.
69. John Beresford (ed.), *The Diary of a Country Parson: the Reverend James Woodforde* (London: Oxford UP, 1924–31), vol. 2, pp. 68–69, and vols 1–3, passim.
70. See the 'Poultry' chapter, in Isabella Beeton, *The Book of Household Management* (1861; facs. repr. entitled *Beeton's Book of Household Management*, London: Chancellor, 1997), pp. 443–506.

CHAPTER SIX

'A PUDDING HAS TWO ENDS':
BOILED PUDDINGS THROUGH THE AGES

Laura Mason

Asixteenth-century proverb, 'Every thing hath an end and a pudding hath two', refers to the sausage-like forms which puddings took at that time. However, a brief examination of later usages of the word 'pudding' in English reveals an extraordinarily complex subject provoking circular discussions rather than an end of any description. Individual recipes can be savoury or sweet, cooked by moist methods (boiling, steaming) or dry ones (baking); they can be everyday, simple dishes or elaborate presentations for special occasions, such as plum (Christmas) pudding. As a class of food, 'pudding' is used to indicate the final, sweet course of a meal, roughly equivalent to dessert, but some types are emphatically not sweet, involving, or being firmly associated with, the meat course. At least one, Yorkshire pudding, may be served before meat at the start of a meal, with meat in the archetypal English combination of 'roast beef and Yorkshire', and is also, occasionally, eaten after meat with syrup as a kind of dessert. The world of puddings is full of exceptions and contradictions, and the English language seems to use it as a catch-all for dishes which European cuisines have equivalents for but do not put into one general category.

Apart from this, there are colloquial non-food usages of the word, including 'in the pudding club' for being pregnant, and several other proverbs. 'The proof of the pudding is in the eating' has been in use since the seventeenth century and is is still current. There is no space in this paper to explore all nuances of the word, or all associated dishes; I am more concerned with early recipes, a few items of kitchen equipment associated with them, and dishes descended from them.

DEFINITIONS

Because of the complexity of the subject, there is no satisfactory general definition of pudding as a foodstuff. In the late nineteenth century, Theodore Garrett remarked despairingly in the *Encyclopaedia of Practical Cookery*:

The term [pudding] itself ... is in culinary parlance extended so widely by the fancies and tastes of cooks that it is difficult to assign any limitation to its application. Webster describes a Pudding as a species of food of a soft or moderately hard consistency variously made, and this we are compelled to accept, having nothing more definite to offer.[1]

The *Oxford English Dictionary* incorporated part of this into its 1989 definition of pudding:

A preparation of food of a soft or moderately firm consistency, in which the ingredients, animal or vegetable, are either mingled in a farinaceous basis (chiefly of flour), or are enclosed in a farinaceous 'crust' .... and cooked by boiling or steaming. Preparations of batter, milk and eggs, rice, sago, tapioca, and other farinaceous substances, suitably seasoned, and cooked by baking, are now also called puddings.[2]

The earliest reference for this usage is given as 1544. However, the editors regard this as the second major definition of pudding. Their first major definition has three food-related aspects: as the stomach or entrails of an animal stuffed with meat and other ingredients, boiled (first citation *c.* 1305); as a stuffing roasted in the belly cavity of a whole animal (1596); and as the entrails themselves (1444). These meanings have much more explicitly visceral connections, as has a specific type of pudding, the haggis, first described in print around 1420.[3]

The *OED* points to a probable but unproven relationship of the word pudding with the French *boudin*, a distinct lack of any certain derivation for either term, and considers any connection with Latin *botulus* (sausage) difficult, whilst acknowledging that *boldone*, a more closely related Italian word is recorded. Instead, the editors look towards Germanic dialect words related to the idea of swelling.

Behind the uncertain etymology, there is, perhaps, a more explicit association between puddings or *boudins* and offal. A Tuscan name for both black puddings and cleaned, salted and dried pig's intestines is *budino*.[4] The idea of stuffing also sometimes suggests innards. Stuffing, or force-meat, as a seasoned mixture of meat, fat and cereal, is not that distant from offal pudding mixtures, and early recipes for some creature – a fish, a lamb, a pig – cooked 'with a pudding in its belly', i.e., stuffed, recall the gruesome visual trick played on the guests in the Roman text 'Trimalchio's Feast', involving a roast pig, whose belly spilled out sausages when slit. Beneath the semantics of puddings, obscured by the niceties which insulate food on the table from visceral origins, a culinary association between puddings and guts certainly exists.

In modern European languages, the *OED* considers the word pudding to be taken from the current English sense relating to texture and associated with dessert. The editors remain silent on Iberian usage, a comparison which might have been interesting. Alan Davidson observed that whilst there is no exact translation of pudding (in its current English sense) in other European languages, that 'the Portuguese *pudim* (and to a lesser extent the Spanish *púding*) are similar concepts'.[5]

This does nothing to explain the prominence of puddings and pudding generally in English food habits, something which may be more related to use than recipes and methods. Whether pudding was simply one dish among many, or whether it had other connotations as a staple is not clear, and probably varied according to wealth and class. Poorer people, especially, may have relied on offal puddings as sources of animal protein, and perhaps emphasized the cereal component by increasing this in proportion to scarcer, more expensive ingredients. A much-quoted passage from the French traveller Henri Misson about the ubiquity, variety and excellence of puddings served at English dinners suggests that they were a standard part of the meal in the late seventeenth century; he also comments that the English ate much meat and little bread, and cites a saying about 'pudding time' as an expression for an opportune moment.[6] Gilly Lehmann (2003) remarks that Misson was writing with overtones of irony, implying that his comment was not as flattering to puddings as it seems in the 1719 English translation.[7] The idea of pudding as a staple around this time is also remarked on, in conjunction with meat, by William Ellis (1750) who wrote that:

> Pudding is so necessary a part of an Englishman's food that it and beef are accounted the victuals they most love. Pudding is so natural to our harvest-men, that without it they think they cannot make an agreeable dinner.[8]

Lehmann remarks that the plainer types of pudding tended to appear in the first course of menus around this time. The notion of pudding as a first-course filler before the (more expensive) beef is still present in the Yorkshire saying 'them as ets most pudding gets most meat'.[9] During the seventeenth century several types of pudding showed a tendency to develop richer and sweeter versions, and a rapid expansion of sweet (dessert type) is detectable by the end of the century, but flavour category was not an issue at this time. In contemporary British food culture pudding or 'pud' (sweet, conflated with the dessert course) is intrinsic to the definition of a proper meal,[10] but even now a pudding may be savoury, sweet, or flavour-neutral, as the maker pleases.

THE CHARACTERISTICS OF PUDDINGS

When good King Arthur ruled this land
He was a goodly king,
He stole three pecks of barley meal,
To make a bag pudding.

A bag pudding the king did make,
And stuffed it well with plums,
And in it put great lumps of fat,
As big as my two thumbs.

The King and Queen did eat thereof,
And noblemen beside,
And what they could not eat that night,
The Queen next morning fried.

This nursery rhyme (first published in 1872) mentions the use of meal (cereal), fat, and 'plums' (dried fruit); a container, in the form of a bag; and the fact that the pudding was eaten hot, either immediately after making, or reheated. A case can be made for puddings generally (even sweet baked ones) sharing some characteristics beyond the consistency. These are centred around a basic set of ingredients, which at its simplest is fat plus starch plus spice and flavours; the use of specialized containers; and a certain rotundity in shape conferred by these.

Amongst the fats associated with puddings over the centuries are chopped pork fat, beef suet, bone marrow, butter or cream; in the starch category, breadcrumbs, wheat flour, cornflour, oatmeal, rice, barley or dried peas. Spices and flavours vary according to custom, taste and means and extend from the simplest of seasonings to encompass meat or offal, vegetables, herbs, fresh fruit, dried fruit and sugar (both of the latter are sometimes quoted in otherwise savoury, meat-based products). At one time, the herb pennyroyal was closely associated with puddings and a seventeenth-century name for it was 'pudding grass'. Sir Kenelm Digby explains that, this, with thyme and other herbs, made plain bag puddings more savoury, and that little is required, 'but onley to quicken the other flat Ingredients'.[11]

Containers include animal casings which appear to have been used since time immemorial. The alimentary tract of a slaughtered animal provided various convenient, if somewhat linear, edible containers in which to keep bits of offal, meat or fat. A progression in both edible and inedible containers can be detected, from animal casings to pastry of different types, or to inedible cloths, basins and dishes, and the idea of a container often seems to have been an intrinsic part of the pudding. Pudding cloths are sometimes quoted as a distinctively English piece of cookery technology. The container confers an essentially rounded shape – sausage-like, spherical, a rounded cone, an oval. Puddings do not have corners.

Having said this, it is immediately necessary and typical of the subject to declare an exception. This is the hasty-pudding, common from at least the late sixteenth until the nineteenth century. At its most basic it was a simple mixture of milk and meal or flour, boiled to thicken it. Sometimes it was put into a bag or bowls and boiled further, but casings or containers were often dispensed with, the final product being amorphous.[12] This seems more akin to cereal-based staples such as porridge, pottage and polenta, and the relationship (if any) between these and other puddings is obscure. Fat and additions such as sugar were sometimes added at the point of serving. There is no space here to explore this, except to say the simple form appears to have been widespread in early-modern England and to have been eaten especially by the poor. It also appears to have influenced the development of contemporary American ideas about packaged cornflour pudding mixes, and one might speculate if, somewhere along the line, mashed potato (also pale, bland, starchy and amorphous, as well as being a one-time ingredient for richer puddings) got classified into a similar culinary niche.

BLACK PUDDINGS AND OTHER SAUSAGE-TYPE PUDDINGS

Perhaps it is no accident that one of the earliest surviving recipes for puddings is for a black pudding. These products, ancient and widespread in European cookery traditions, have all the characteristics of pudding in general including the basics of cereal, fat and seasoning, and a casing. They also have a limiting factor, the addition of blood, which gives the black colour and needs cereal and fat to produce the moderately firm consistency and a cohesive texture, both of which may relate to keeping-quality as well as to palatability. This fifteenth-century century recipe is for a porpoise pudding:

> Puddying of purpaysse. – Take þe Blode of hym, & þe grece of hym self, & Ote-mele, & Salt, & Pepir, & Gyngere, & melle þese to-gederys wel, & þan putte þis in þe Gutte of þe purpays, & þan lat it seþe esyli, & not hard, a good whylys; & þan take hym uppe, & broyle hym a lytil, & þan serue forth.[13]

To twenty-first century eyes, porpoise meat is not the most obvious food choice, and perhaps this recipe was recorded because it was a courtly, fast-day version of an otherwise common dish in medieval England.

In theory the blood of any food animal could be used; sheep's blood is specified by Thomas Dawson in 1596–7, but black puddings are most closely associated with pigs, as were other types of sausage-shaped offal puddings. 'Of the inward of beasts are made Puddings, which are best of an hog' observed Thomas Cogan in 1584,[14] despite the opinion of physicians that the blood of any beast or fowl was 'hard of dygestyon', as was offal generally.[15] Printed sources from the late sixteenth century onwards show other types including liver or hog's puddings, and white puddings. As the name suggests, the former were made of liver, specifically that of the pig. This recipe was recorded by John Evelyn:

> The Wootton reciet for liver puddings such as they call folks puddings. Take halfe a peck of flower strew some carraway seeds finly bruised cloves mace nutmegs beat fine a little salt grate the liver of a Hogge which has ben boyled in Water with the fatt of the Gutts and crow [mesentery] of fatt which when well boyled must be choped small the kernells and skins picked out and with the fatt and some of the liquor mingle the flower to a tender past put in allso 6 Eggs 3 whites the chiefe moistning must be the fatt … and so cram them into the great gutts boyle them well, after this may be kept in the Chimney hung up they are so sliced and fried when eaten.[16]

That Evelyn called them folk's puddings suggests that this was essentially a rural, rustic product. Dawson (1596) gives a similar recipe, but calls it hog's pudding.

White pudding recipes were more varied. Oatmeal, bread, rice, barley and almonds provided the basis, and fine ingredients such as rosewater, ambergris, sugar, cream and bone marrow are sometimes mentioned. An interesting recipe is given in *The Compleat Cook* (1655):

The Lord Conway, his Lordship's Receipt for the making of Amber Puddings. First take the guts of a young Hog, and wash them very clean, and then take two pound of the best Hogs fat, and a pound and a half of the best Jorden Almonds, the which being blancht, take one half of them & beat them very small, & the other half reserve whole unbeaten, then take a pound and a half of fine Sugar, and four white loaves, & grate the loaves over the former composition, and mingle them well together in a Bason, having so done put to it half an ounce of Ambergreece, the which must be scraped very small over the said composition, take half a quarter of an ounce of Levant Musk, and bruise it in a marble Mortar, with a quarter of a pint of Orange-flour water, then mingle these all very well together, and having so done, fill the said Guts therewith. This Receipt was given his Lordship by an Italian for a great rarity, and has been found so to be by those Ladies of honour, to whom his Lordship has imparted the said Reception.[17]

The presence of perfumes, whilst not untypical of sweetened seventeenth-century dishes, adds a touch of status and just possibly, aphrodisiac overtones, whilst the generally exotic air is completed by the attribution to an Italian. Flesh is not involved except in the form of a relatively low proportion of pig fat and the actual casings. The use of almonds and the high sugar content anticipates recipes for baked almond puddings in the eighteenth century, a development route which white puddings in general seem to have followed.

Jos. Cooper, who in 1654 styled himself chief cook to the late king (Charles I), recorded about twenty pudding recipes, including black, oatmeal and white puddings, with several rich and perfumed variants on the almond, rice or barley theme. Colour contrasts between the varieties appear to have been valued. The status of offal puddings generally is not clear and probably depended much on the ingredients; the seventeenth century saying that 'he who seldom eats meat thinks pudding a treat' suggests a certain disdain, at least among those whose food was abundant.

By the early eighteenth century, the ingredients used as a basis for white puddings were all favoured for baked puddings, discussed in the next chapter by Fiona Lucraft. Also, a gradual change in the classification of offal puddings began. Recipes for black puddings, and various sausage-type white, liver or hog puddings (the categories showed a tendency to elide into each other) are common in cookery books from the seventeenth and early eighteenth centuries. In the mid-eighteenth century, Hannah Glasse still gave recipes for hog's puddings and black puddings, together in a section with sausages. Eventually recipes for hog's and black puddings disappear from most recipe books, perhaps a reflection of a growing urban middle-class, less interested in the practicalities of killing and preparing pigs for household consumption. Rural families and poorer people must have continued to make and appreciate them.

Black puddings are still widely available, often encountered as part of the 'full English' breakfast, and particularly associated with the food habits of south Lancashire. Recipes have remained essentially unchanged, although the demise of domestic pig-killing and public hygiene regulations have concentrated manufacture in the hands of specialists. Their geographical spread and temporal persistence must relate in part to their suitability as a use for animal blood.[18] The paler puddings are also available in places. Twenty-first-century versions of hog's puddings can still be bought in south-western England, although liver no longer seems to be an ingredient. Scotland has oat-based mealy (oatmeal) puddings and 'fruity' puddings (of suet, cereal and dried fruit). It is possible they have also influenced British notions about sausages. A subliminal link between the idea of a pudding and a sausage would help to explain (though not necessarily excuse) the commercial British sausage containing bread or rusk. Products such as this were a logical use for scraps of meat, fat and offal which might otherwise go to waste, something unthinkable in a subsistence economy. But fine white sausage-type puddings have vanished from British tradition (unlike France where the *boudin blanc* is still available), leaving as their only representatives baked rice, sago or bread puddings with no obvious relationship to their sausage-like precursors.

HAGGISES AND BAG PUDDINGS

Haggises, a specialized type of pudding of minced offal, fat, cereal, and spices stuffed into the cleaned maw (stomach) of an animal, also have a long history. The current recipe, based on sheep offal and oatmeal, has remained remarkably consistent since the first record of it in the fifteenth century. They are now associated with Scotland to the extent that they have become a Scottish national symbol, but this appears to be relatively recent. In the seventeenth century, haggises were more widely made. For instance in 1654, Jos. Cooper included 'haggus-puddings' amongst his recipes:

> Take a Calves Chaldron [intestines], being well scoured and par-boyled, and the kernels taken out, and when it is cold mince it very small; then take four or five Eggs, and leave out halfe the whites, and take thick Creame, grated Bread, Sugar, Nutmeg, Salt Currans and Rosewater, and (if you will) Sweet-majerome, Thyme and Parsley; mix it well together: then having a Sheeps Maw [stomach] ready dressed, put it in, and boyle it a little: remember Suet or Marrow.[19]

This courtly recipe may not much resemble the sheep and oatmeal offering, but the presence of bread, sugar, currants and suet is interesting in view of the later popularity of these ingredients in English puddings, and the use of a maw gave a rounded rather than sausage form. Haggises gradually vanished from English food tradition, but the idea of roundness did not, and was enhanced by an innovation: the pudding cloth. Jos. Cooper mentions this as one among several items used for boiled pudding mixtures at this time; guts, maws, the cloth (sometimes double), and bags; in one case his instructions say to fill a mixture into guts but then notes 'or I think it will do well in a bag',[20] suggesting that the two were becoming interchangeable.

It is unclear when the use of a cloth, or a cloth bag as containers for puddings originated. They are first mentioned around the start of the seventeenth century, for instance in John Murrell's recipe for 'A Cambridge Pudding', first published in 1617:

> Searce grated bread thorow a cullinder, mince it with Flower, minst Dates, Currans, Nutmeg, Sinamon & Pepper, minst Suet, new milk warme, fine

Sugar and Egs: take away some of their whites, worke all together. Take halfe the Pudding on the one side, and the other on the other side, and make it round like a loafe. Then take Butter, and put it in the midst of the Pudding, and the other halfe aloft. Let your liquor boyle, and throw your pudding in, being tyed in a faire cloth: when it is boyled enough cut it in the middest, and so serue it in.[21]

Murrell's Cambridge pudding both appears to be the basic model for later recipes for boiled suet puddings, and gives a clear instruction for using a cloth. C. Anne Wilson observed that:

The invention of the pudding-cloth or bag finally severed the link between puddings and animal guts. Puddings could now be made at any time, and they became a regular part of the daily fare of almost all classes.[22]

How intestines or maws came to be replaced by cloths is unclear. Wilson points out that they were only available when an animal had been killed. They were single-use, eaten or discarded after cooking. Also, perhaps, because animal-derived membranes had a tendency to break during boiling, allowing the pudding mixture to escape, the idea of wrapping a cloth round a caul or haggis was seen as a fail-safe arrangement. John Evelyn, for instance, gave a recipe for a calf's foot pudding which was to be wrapped in the caul of a breast of veal – that is, the parchment-like membrane which covers it – and then in a cloth.[23] An earlier recipe from Dawson, discussed more fully by Fiona Lucraft, below, requires a pudding to be wrapped in a caul and then in pastry and baked, suggesting that the animal membrane was still viewed as an essential part of a pudding when cloths and pastry wrappings for puddings were at the innovative stage. Maws and cauls were dispensed with, but pudding cloths remained a favoured piece of English kitchen technology up to the twentieth century; and pastry, both as baked puff or shortcrust types, and as wet-cooked suet paste, became an intrinsic part of many puddings.

QUAKING PUDDINGS, BATTER AND PUDDING MOULDS

Wilson also discusses how animal-derived membranes must also have been rather unequal to a specific pudding type which was exceptionally popular between the seventeenth and nineteenth centuries: the quaking puddings, based on very liquid batters. This type of pudding is implicated in a recipe recorded at the very start of the seventeenth century, 'To make a bagge pudinge' in Hilary Spurling's transcription of Elinor Fettiplace's receipt book, a manuscript dated to 1604:

> Take thicke Creame and make yt somewhat hotter then bloud warme, then take halfe a dossen egges and beate them well and mingle them wth yor Creame then ad to yt a little parsely and winter savory cut very smale and some nutmegges suger and a little salte then put to yt as much Crumes of bread and fine flower as will make yt thicker then Batter for pan-Cakes, then wett yor bagge in cold water and put yt in and when yor water boyles put him into yt, yt must not bee boyled wth meate but alone in fayre water.[24]

It is not absolutely explicit that a cloth is intended here (in some dialects bag is a word for stomach), but the direction to wet it in cold water suggests a cloth. It is clear that a fairly liquid, and therefore potentially troublesome, mixture was being dealt with. By the mid-seventeenth century, Jos. Cooper makes it clear that he used a cloth, buttered and floured, for a batter 'shaking pudding'.[25] Although bags were commonly used for these, a less porous type of container could be an advantage. Jos. Cooper hints at the use of earthernware containers in an instruction which apparently relates to reheating rice pudding: 'put them in pipkins and boyl them for eating,'[26] but it is Sir Kenelm Digby (1669) who shows how the pudding basin might have originated. His 'good Quaking Bag-pudding' required milk with nutmeg, breadcrumbs, egg yolks, butter, sugar and a little sack, muscadine or amber-flavoured sugar, but no bag. After mixing, he directs:

> Then put this mixtion into a deep Woodden dish (like a great Butter-box) which must first be on the inside a little greased with Butter, and a little Flower sprinkled thereon, to save the Pudding from sticking to the sides of the dish. Then put a linnen cloth or handkercher over the mouth of the

dish, and reverse the mouth downwards, so that you may tye the Napkin close with two knots by the corners cross, or with a strong thred, upon the bottom of the dish, then turned upwards; all which is, that the matter may not get out, and yet the boiling water get through the linnen upon it on one side enough to bake the pudding sufficiently. Put the Woodden-dish thus filled and tyed up into a great Possnet or little Kettle of boiling water. The faster it boils, the better it will be. The dish will turn and rowl up and down in the water, as it gallopeth in boiling. An hours boiling is sufficient. Then unty your linnen, and take it off, and reverse the mouth of the dish downwards into the Silver-dish you will serve it up in; wherein is sufficient melted Butter thickened with beating, and sweetened to your taste with Sugar, to serve for Sauce. You may beat a little Sack or Muscadine, or Rose, or Orange-flower-water with the Sauce.[27]

This is the earliest reference I have so far been able to find to something clearly approximating to the pudding basin. Digby's careful instructions suggest it was not the most usual way of boiling a pudding, but by the early eighteenth century several instructions for boiling mixtures in wooden dishes can be found. John Nott (1726) gives two examples, one of which, 'Puddings of several Colours' requires 'half a dozen wooden Dishes with Covers to them', each filled with a portion of quaking pudding mixture coloured a different colour with spinach, cowslips, etc., the lids tied down with cloths before boiling. The cooked puddings were taken out of the bowls, stuck with suckets and served with butter, vinegar, rose-water and sugar poured over them.[28] E. Smith, in *The Compleat Housewife* (first published in 1727) also cited the use of pottery dishes for boiled puddings, such as 'To make Hasty Puddings, to boil in Custard Dishes':

Take a large pint of milk, put to it four spoonfuls of flour; mix it well together, set it over the fire, and boil it into a smooth hasty pudding; sweeten it to your taste, grate nutmeg in it, and when 'tis almost cold, beat five eggs very well, and stir into it; then butter your custard-cups, put in your stuff, and tie them over with a cloth, put them in the pot when the water boils, and let them boil something more than half an hour; pour on them melted butter.[29]

It is not clear if the cups were completely submerged, but with their cloth covers, they must have looked like modern pudding basins. In *The Complete Practical Cook* (1730), Charles Carter suggests either baking or boiling for many of his pudding recipes, and he cited dishes for boiling some of them. Hannah Glasse (1747) repeats a version of Nott's recipe, as 'Puddings for little Dishes', instructing the cook to make four little ones in different colours, and one larger white one, and to 'tye your Covers over very close with Pack-thread …when enough, turn them out in a Dish, the white One in the Middle, and the four coloured ones round.'[30] A version of the turreted and crenellated custard mould of the nineteenth century can be glimpsed in these instructions. Glasse also gives a paragraph on 'Rules to be observed in making Puddings, &c', in which she mentions both wooden bowls and china dishes as containers.[31] Boiled batter puddings faded from use in the nineteenth century, although in baked form they soldier on as Yorkshire pudding, and the idea of quaking-pudding has recently been revived by the chef Heston Blumenthal.

SUET PUDDINGS, BOILING AND STEAMING

Glasse's classification of puddings is interesting. She puts some in a separate section, possibly intending them to be seen as accompaniments for meat. Amongst them is a recipe for boiled plum pudding, similar to modern recipes, and early citations for 'a boiled suet pudding' and for 'a Stake-Pudding', both subsequently common in the English kitchen. The latter is recognizable as the ancestor of a steak-and-kidney pudding:

> Make a good Crust with Suet shread fine with Flour, and mix it up with cold Water. Season it with a little Salt, and make a pretty stiff Crust, about two Pounds of Suet, to a Quarter of a Peck of Flour. Let your Stakes be either Beef or Mutton, well seasoned with Pepper and Salt, make it up as you do an Apple-pudding, tye it in a Cloth, and put it in the Water boiling. If it be a large Pudding, it will take five Hours; if a small one, three Hours. This is the best Crust for a Apple-pudding. Pigeons eat well this way.[32]

To find out how to make it up like the apple pudding, one has to turn to the section on dishes 'for a Fast dinner' where one is instructed to make a puff-paste (more usually used for baked puddings), fill it with pared and cored apples, close it up and tie it in a cloth for boiling. 'A Pear Pudding make the same way. And thus you may make a Damson Pudding, or any sort of Plumbs, Apricots, Cherries, or Mulberries, and are very fine.'[33] Pastry puddings enclosing fruit or meat fillings were also sometimes called dumplings, an area of language and cookery which is not investigated here.

The recipes and techniques outlined in the sections above lay the basis for boiled puddings generally over the next two centuries. But when did people begin to steam puddings, as opposed to boiling them? In the late eighteenth and early nineteenth centuries, Elizabeth Raffald and Maria Rundell were still boiling puddings. However, in 1824, John Conrad Cooke makes a distinction in methods:

> This is done two ways, which ought to be particularly attended to; the first is by immersing them totally in boiling water; the second by steaming them in a balnea marie or water-bath; this is done by placing the mould or basin in a stew-pan, with hot water just sufficient to boil it without boiling over.
>
> All liquid puddings should be boiled this way, as they are apt to be spoiled if the water gets to them; particularly boiled souffle, custard, muffins and light puddings.
>
> [...] Note. – The common tin steamer is of particular use, and most convenient for these purposes.[34]

Eliza Acton thought that batter was much lighter boiled in a cloth than a mould, and plum pudding 'which it is customary to boil in moulds' was lighter and less dry when boiled in cloths, but goes on to say 'Many persons prefer their puddings steamed'.[35]

Acton also shows an innovative approach to savoury suet puddings, a 'purely English class of dishes' which tended (because of fashion), to have been 'confined ... almost entirely to the simple family dinners of the middle classes'. Her recipes sound delicious: venison with truffles, sweetbreads with oysters or button mushrooms; pheasants, partridges, moorfowl, woodcocks, snipes, plovers, wheatears or veal kidneys, but she remarks that eels (and sausages and harslet) were 'unsuited to delicate eaters.'[36] (Haslet – the pluck of a pig – recalls a recipe given in 1654 by Jos. Cooper for a pudding of swine-lights.) In her recipe for 'beef-steak, or John Bull's pudding' she provides a clue to its popularity in some households, saying that it is 'often in great esteem with sportsmen, ... as an additional hour's boiling, or even more, will have little effect on a large pudding of this kind.'[37]

Some item similar to the modern pudding basin obviously existed by this time, as Acton also states that:

> All meat puddings are more conveniently made in deep pans, moulds or basins having a thick rim, below which the cloths can be tied without the hazard of their slipping off; and as the puddings should by no means be turned out before they are sent to table, one to match the dinner-service, at least in colour, is desirable.[38]

She notes that some families used shallow pie or tart dishes for boiling puddings, and that 'In Kent and Sussex, shallow pans in form somewhat resembling a large deep saucer, are sold expressly for boiling meat puddings.'[39] This area appears to have been especially rich in pudding recipes. 'Well' or 'pond' puddings with butter and sugar in the middle (remiscent of Murrell's seventeenth-century college pudding) were also associated with this area, the best-known modern version being the Sussex pond pudding.

By the mid-nineteenth century, suet puddings had developed into considerable variety, eaten by all classes. Francatelli (1852) records some plain versions suitable for the working class, including one with treacle mixed into the paste, jam roll pudding (the rolled or bolster type of pudding which became known as jam roly-poly), a savoury roll pudding filled with bacon, onion and apple, and a rabbit pudding.[40] Very plain suet puddings were often disliked by the children they were inflicted on in school or nursery and gained numerous uncomplimentary nicknames.

SPONGE PUDDINGS

Sponge pudding, familiar to anyone raised in Britain before the 1970s, is something of a parvenu. The earliest recipe found during research for this paper was in Eliza Acton's book, where this recipe for 'Prince Albert's Pudding' appears:

Beat to a cream half a pound of fresh butter and mix with it by degrees an equal weight of pounded loaf-sugar, dried and sifted; add to these, after they have been well beaten together, first the yolks, and then the whites of five fresh eggs, which have been thoroughly whisked apart; now strew lightly in, half a pound of the finest flour, dried and sifted, and last of all, half a pound of jar raisins, weighed after they are stoned. Put these ingredients, perfectly mixed, into a well-buttered mould, or floured cloth, and boil the pudding for three hours... We recommend a little pounded mace, or the grated rind of a small lemon, to vary the flavour of this excellent pudding; and that when a mould is used, slices of candied peel should be laid rather thickly over it after it is buttered.[41]

Steaming became the norm for sponge puddings in twentieth-century practice. The popularity of this type of pudding may have been increased by manufacturers of baking powder and flour millers via the leaflets they issued to promote their products, with additions of jam, syrup, dried fruit, lemon or cocoa, much as sponge cakes were elaborated at the end of the nineteenth century.

PLUM PUDDINGS

Many details relating to pudding recipes and customs remain obscure. One is exactly how the Christmas pudding developed; the general theory is that it was a conflation of the Cambridge-type suet pudding with the heavily fruited, meaty Christmas pottage of an earlier tradition. No evidence to contradict this has come to light, nor has anything obviously supporting the theory. Just as some white puddings seem to have freed themselves of the constraints of casings or cloths, it is not impossible to imagine the reverse taking place. Both plum pudding and plum pottage occur in the early eighteenth century, and some types of plum or other suet pudding appear to have been routinely served with roast beef.[42] Plum puddings were not an exclusively Christmas food in the eighteenth century, although they had associations with special occasions. William Ellis (1750), continuing his discussion about the essential role of pudding in the diet of the Englisman, told how

Therefore in Hertfordshire our rule is, to make plumb-pudding during wheat harvest [...] and plain pudding during the rest of the time. Now to make a plumb-pudding of the better sort for six harvest-mens dinners, our housewife makes use of a pottle of flower, a quart of skim or new milk, three eggs, half or three quarters of a pound of raisins, and half a pound of chopt suet. [...] Boil it three or (better) four hours; and if they cannot dine on this with good boiled beef, or with pork, or with bacon and roots, or herbs, they deserve to want a dinner.[43]

From the eighteenth century onwards, the English took plum pudding wherever they went, and it became steadily more embedded in the notion of Britishness. The spherical shape meant it could represent the whole world. James Gillray's cartoon *The Plum-Pudding in Danger* (c. 1800) shows Napoleon and William Pitt cutting up a pudding with a map of the world over the surface. In 1814, the Parisian chef Beauvilliers gave a recipe for 'plumbuting', presumably for English, or British, tastes. During the British Raj it was introduced to India, where a version was recorded as 'Madras Club Pudding'. It also developed an attachment to Christmas. In 1850, the *Illustrated London News* asserted that

the plum pudding is a national symbol. It does not represent a class or caste, but the bulk of the English nation. There is not a man, woman or child raised above what the French would call *prolétaires*, that does not expect a taste of plum pudding of some sort or another on Christmas Day.[44]

A few years later the same paper depicted Indian soldiers at Jalalabad eating their Christmas pudding.[45] In the 1920s, a campaign to encourage trade within the British Empire led to eventually to 'An Empire Christmas Pudding', included in a collection of recipes with royal associations published by Elizabeth Craig in 1953:

5lb Australian currants, 5lb Australian sultanas, 5lb South African stoned raisins, 1 ½ lb minced Canadian apples, 5lb United Kingdom breadcrumbs, 5lb New Zealand beef suet, 2lb South African cut candied peel, 2 ½ lb United Kingdom flour, 2 ½ lb West Indies Demerara sugar, 20 eggs (Irish Free State), 2oz Ceylon ground cinnamon, 1 ½ oz Zanzibar ground cloves, 1 ½ oz ground nutmegs (Straits Settlements), 1 tsp Indian pudding spice,

¼ pint Cyprus brandy, ½ pint Jamaica rum, 2 quarts Old English beer.

Place all the dry ingredients in a basin. Mix well and add the eggs, stirring well. Add the liquid and stir to mix thoroughly, Press into greased pudding basins. Steam for six hours and when required, steam again for six hours.[46]

The Empire has diminished, and consumption of plum puddings now appears to be limited to the time immediately around Christmas, though whether there is any link between the two phenomena is unprovable. Suet and steamed puddings generally seem to have declined in popularity, and ideas to do with the unhealthiness of animal fats, the time required to cook them, and a taste for lighter foods have probably all influenced this.

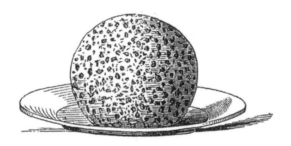

CONCLUSION

Attempting to unravel some of the history and meanings of the word pudding gives one great sympathy for the dictionary compilers quoted in the introduction to this chapter. If there is not already a collective noun for puddings, I should like to propose 'a confusion' as an appropriate term. They are generally a complex subject. The early history and constrained form of some types is obscured by the extraordinary variety of later techniques, several of which seem to have developed fully during the seventeenth century, and the numerous recipes associated with pudding.

Boiled puddings had a long career as both fine food and boring fillers, and a role as plain poverty food and staples of institutional catering in the nineteenth and twentieth centuries did them no favours. Plum pudding, a favoured festive dish from the eighteenth to mid-twentieth centuries has now become confined to Christmas, and other sweet steamed suet puddings have slipped from favour, although they can be excellent. Savoury puddings appear to be confined to the well-loved classic form of steak and kidney pudding, but so deep is the affection for this that in 2001 Marks and Spencer test-marketed a vegetarian equivalent, filled with mushroom and roast onions. Anything 'traditional' which develops a non-meat analogue resonates very deeply for the English. But it is the more generalized concept of puddings as dessert that continues to flourish and adapt. This is the context in which most people now tend to think of them, and the one which will be examined in the next chapter.

NOTES

1. Theodore Francis Garrett, *c.* 1895, quoted by Alan Davidson, *The Penguin Companion to Food* (London: Penguin Books, 2002), p. 765.

2. *Oxford English Dictionary* (2nd edition, 1989).

3. In the *Liber Cocorum*, quoted in the *OED* (2nd edition, 1989) under Haggis.

4. Elizabeth Romer, *The Tuscan Year* (London: Weidenfeld and Nicolson, 1984), p. 14.

5. Alan Davidson, *The Penguin Companion to Food* (London: Penguin Books, 2002), p. 765.

6. Henri Misson, trans. Ozell, *Mr Misson's Memoirs and Observations in his Travel over England with some Account of Scotland and Ireland* (1719).

7. Gilly Lehmann, *The British Housewife* (Blackawton: Prospect Books, 2003), p. 198.

8. William Ellis, *The Country Housewife's Family Companion*, from the edition of 1750 with an introduction by Malcolm Thick (Blackawton: Prospect Books, 2000), p. 78.

9. For a discussion of the development of Yorkshire pudding and customs associated with it, see Jennifer Stead, 'Prodigal Frugality: Yorkshire Pudding and Parkin, two traditional Yorkshire foods' in C. Anne Wilson, ed., *Traditional Food East and West of the Pennines* (Edinburgh: Edinburgh University Press, 1991), pp. 143–156.

10. For mid-twentieth-century ideas about this, see Michael Nicod, 'Gastronomically Speaking: Food Studied as a Medium of Communication' in Michael Turner, ed., *Nutrition and Lifestyles* (London: Applied Science Publishers, 1980).

11. Peter Davidson and Jane Stevenson, eds., *The Closet of Sir Kenelme Digby Kt Opened* (Blackawton: Prospect Books, 1997), p. 149. Pennyroyal, *Mentha pulegium*, is a seasoning persistently associated with black puddings in England; curiously, thousands of miles to the east in Afghanistan, this herb is known as *pudina*. See Helen Saberi, *Noshe Djan* (Blackawton: Prospect Books, 1986), p. 36.

12. Even so, Jos. Cooper, *The Art of Cookery Refin'd and Augmented* (1654), gives a recipe 'To make a hasty pudding in a bag', p. 142.

13. Thomas Austin, ed., *Two fifteenth-century cookery-books* (London: Early English Text Society, O.S. 91. 1888), p. 42.

14. Quoted by Linda and Roger Flavell, *Dictionary of Proverbs and their Origins* (London: Kyle Cathie, 1993), p. 200.

15. F.J. Furnivall, ed., *A Compendyous Regyment or A Dyetary of Helth compiled by Andrew Boorde* (London: Early English Text Society, 1870), p. 276.

16. Christopher Driver, ed., *John Evelyn, Cook: the manuscript recipe book of John Evelyn* (Blackawton: Prospect Books, 1997), p. 137.

17. *The Compleat Cook* (London: 1655), p. 99. See the facsimile edition of *The Compleat Cook and a Queens Delight* (London: Prospect Books, 1984).

18. It is not essential to make these into sausage type products, and in places the mixture is baked in a dish, but this is unusual.

19. Cooper, op. cit ., pp. 139–40.

20. Cooper, op. cit., p. 144.

21. John Murrel, *A New Book of Cookerie* (London: 1617). See the facsimile of the 1634 edition (Ilkley: Jacksons of Ilkley, 1985), p. 44.

22. C. Anne Wilson, *Food and Drink in Britain* (London: Constable, 1973), p. 316.

23. Driver, op. cit., p. 55.

24. Hilary Spurling, *Elinor Fettiplace's Receipt Book* (London: Penguin, 1986), p. 46.

25. Cooper, op. cit., p. 142.

26. Cooper, op. cit., p. 147.

27. Davidson and Stevenson, op. cit., p. 148–9.

28. John Nott, *Cooks and Confectioners Dictionary* (London: 1726). See the facsimile edition (London: Lawrence Rivington, 1980) with an introduction and glossary by Elizabeth David,

p. 245, 'To make puddings of several colours'.

29. E. Smith, *The Compleat Housewife's Companion* (London, 1758, 16th edition). See the facsimile edition (Kings Langley: Arlon House Publishing, 1983), p. 142.

30. Hannah Glasse, *The Art of Cookery Made Plain and Easy by a Lady* (London, 1747). See the facsimile edition (London: Prospect Books, 1983), p. 110.

31. Glasse, op. cit., p. 70.

32. Glasse, op. cit., p. 69.

33. Glasse, op. cit., p. 112.

34. John Conrad Cooke, *Cookery and Confectionary* (London: 1824), p. 104.

35. Eliza Acton, *Modern Cookery for Private Families* (London 1855). See the facsimile edition with an introduction by Elizabeth Ray (Lewes: Southover Press, 1993), p. 334.

36. Acton, op. cit., p. 336.

37. Acton, op. cit., p. 337.

38. Acton, op. cit., p. 336.

39. Acton, op. cit., p. 336.

40. Charles Elmé Francatelli, *A Plain Cookery Book for the Working Classes* (London: Routledge, Warne and Routledge, 1852). See the facsimile edition (London: Scolar Press, 1977).

41. Acton, op. cit., p. 346.

42. Experiments with a rich hunting pudding recipe from Mrs Raffald's *Experienced English Housekeeper* (1782) as an accompaniment to roast beef showed that this could be a delicious combination.

43. Ellis, op. cit., p. 78.

44. Supplement to the *Illustrated London News*, Christmas 1850, p. 485.

45. Supplement to the *Illustrated London News*, February 8th 1879, p. 133.

46. Quoted by Claire Clifton, *The Art of Food* (London: Windward, 1988), p. 110.

CHAPTER SEVEN

GENERAL SATISFACTION:
A HISTORY OF BAKED PUDDINGS

Fiona Lucraft

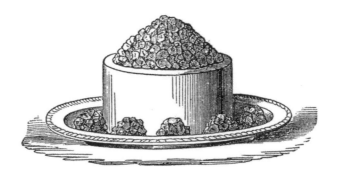

A mongst the array of definitions for puddings offered in dictionaries and cookery books, I like both the succinct wisdom of Dr Johnson and the wordy vagueness of Theodore Francis Garrett:

Pudding: A kind of food very variously compounded, but generally made of meal, milk and eggs.[1]

A Dictionary of the English Language (1755)

The term itself, which, according to Skeat, is of Celtic origin, is in culinary parlance extended so widely by the fancies and tastes of cooks that it is difficult to assign any limitation to its application. Webster describes a Pudding as a species of food of a soft or moderately hard consistency variously made, and this we are compelled to accept, having nothing more definite to offer.[2]

The Encyclopaedia of Practical Cookery (c. 1890)

For the purposes of this paper I suggest a baked pudding fulfils the following requirements; the ingredients include a grain such as wheat, barley, rice and oats used in a variety of forms, e.g. whole-grain, flour, bread. It is enriched with fat in the form of milk, cream, butter or bone marrow. It is lightened, generally with eggs, although yeast and chemical leavening are also used. It can be sweetened and flavoured, e.g. with sugar, spices, fruit and vegetables.

In this paper I will trace the history of baked puddings found in culinary texts from the sixteenth century to the early twentieth century. I will concentrate on the historical development of a generous handful of puddings, some of which are much loved and well remembered, while others have fallen out of favour.

The term 'pudding' gradually came to mean the sweet dishes eaten at the end of a meal and many of the puddings discussed could be found there, but a survey of this final course is not my concern. Nor will I be dealing with the vagaries of the oven or cooking equipment, which have been dealt with elsewhere.[3]

THE SIXTEENTH AND SEVENTEENTH CENTURIES

The first mention of a pudding to be baked, rather than boiled, appears in Thomas Dawson's *The good huswifes Iewell*, published 1596–7. 'A pudding of a Calves Chaldron' may not appeal to the modern cook as it is a dish of cooked entrails thickened with bread and flour, flavoured with spices and preserved orange, then wrapped in a sheep's caul and baked in a 'coffin of fine paste.'[4] The method of mixing all the ingredients together and wrapping them in a protective skin links baked puddings to their older, boiled relatives. Baking the ingredients in a pastry case, evocatively described as a coffin, was the most common method for protecting a dish from the fierce heat of an oven. Coffins of pastry were the original ovenproof dish and countless puddings continued to be made in pastry cases long after alternative containers were created.

John Murrell was the first writer to devote an entire chapter to puddings in the first of his *Two Books of Cookerie and Carving*. The edition I have used is the fifth, of 1638.

Murrell offers a collection of fried, boiled and baked dishes, included amongst the latter are 'A Sierced Pudding', 'A Florentine of Veale', 'A

Fond Pudding', 'Puffes on the English Fashion', 'Italian Pudding' and 'Kickshawes'.[5]

Several of these puddings are recognizable as early mince pies. The 'Sierced Pudding' takes its name from the 'sierced' or sieved bread, which is mixed with minced mutton, dried fruit, candied peel, sweet herbs and warming spices. Like the calves' chaldron recipe, it is wrapped in caul, but the cook has the option of boiling or baking it.

The 'Florentine' is a dish with similar ingredients, which are warmed in a chafing dish before being baked between two sheets of puff paste. Although Murrell gives no instructions for it, a Florentine was a pie with a highly decorative, cut surface.

The 'Fond Pudding' is another dish in the mince pie tradition, containing spicy minced meat, dried fruit and herbs, but is moulded into shapes of 'Birds, Beasts, Fishes, Peares or what you will'. They are fried or baked and served on sippets (toast), along with a sauce of verjuice, or white wine, butter and sugar.

The 'Puffes' were iced cheesecakes and the 'Kickshawes' were little pastries filled with spiced fruit, cheese curds or almond paste. Their name developed from the French '*quelquechose*', implying a little something to eat.

The preferred pastry for baked puddings from the seventeenth to the nineteenth centuries was puff pastry. Murrell gives a recipe in the second of his two books, along with further pudding recipes. This recipe is still recognizable today, as it carefully incorporates butter into folds of pastry. Murrell goes further than modern cooks, by rolling the pastry 12 or more times. He also suggests various fillings, including 'rice, with yolks of eggs, boiled with cream' and 'potato or erringo roots with pieces of marrow rolled in egg and seasoned with cinnamon, sugar, ginger and a very little salt'.[6] These expensive ingredients are a reminder that this book was for the wealthy. Murrell stands out as a helpful writer in an age when cookery books were often compiled for other cooks as memory aids, rather than manuals. He offers guidance in making up the dishes, including how to close and decorate the pastry lid of the puff paste; 'you may cut it crosse the brim of the dish like virginall keyes, and turn them crosse over one another'. He also comments on how the puff paste should look: 'When you see your paste rise up white in the oven, and begin to turne yellow, then take it forth and wash it with rosewater and butter, scrape on fine sugar.'

Murrell sometimes adds when a dish should be served. The 'Puffes' and 'Fond Pudding' are suitable for dinner or supper, while the 'Florentine' is specified for the second course. While puddings can be found in the early part of a dinner, it is more common for writers through the centuries to suggest them for the second half of a meal. Most significant, however, is that one or more puddings would sit alongside other dishes and diners could be expected to eat from a variety of dishes.

ITALIAN PUDDING

Murrell gives two recipes for this pudding, both of which were imitated by many later writers. It was a bread pudding made with distinct cubes of bread mixed with raisins, suet, eggs, sugar, nutmeg and rosewater. Pieces of marrow and dates were stuck decoratively on the top of the dish before baking in a hot oven. In a second recipe, cream and a layer of soft apples are baked under the bread mixture, so changing its texture and flavour.

Murrell's first recipe is similar to one in *A True Gentlewoman's Delight*, published by 'W. J., Gent.' in 1653, and often attributed to Elizabeth, Countess of Kent.[7] The recipe, unlike Murrell's, specifies it will be baked in less than an hour. This telling instruction is repeated in Lord Ruthven's *The Ladies Cabinet Enlarged and Opened* (1654) as well as Robert May's *The Accomplisht Cook* (5th edition 1685). Hannah Wolley gives a recipe in *The Compleat Cook's Guide* (2nd edition 1677) and another in *The Queen-like Closet* (5th edition 1684). William Rabisha also has two recipes in *The Whole Body of Cookery Dissected* (1682 edition); the second of which is entitled 'A Baked Pudding after the Italian Fashion, corrected'. It has clearly developed from Murrell's second recipe with apples. Rabisha gives half a pint of cream for Murrell's four or five spoonfuls, the marrow of two bones for Murrell's five or six lumps and citron is additionally used for decorating the baked pudding.[8] These are slight changes, which nonetheless indicate the gradual clarification of published recipes. In the first half of the eighteenth century Italian Pudding continued to be a popular choice for cookery writers. It is the first recipe in Henry Howard's *England's Newest Way* (3rd edition 1710) and is similar to Murrell's and Rabisha's recipes, but the proportions have changed. Howard adds wine and orange peel to his apples and omits the instruction to dice the bread, so altering its distinctive characteristics. John Nott's recipe in his *Dictionary* of 1726 becomes a pie, with pastry under and over the mix and calls for grated bread. *The Whole Duty of a Woman* (1737), which was later published as *The Lady's Companion* (1740), copies this recipe though uses fewer eggs. Hannah Glasse is known to have used *The Whole Duty of a Woman* for her bestseller, *The Art of Cookery made Plain and Easy* (1747), so it is no surprise to find her Italian pudding mimics the earlier source.[9] Martha Bradley relied on Glasse, *Whole Duty* and Howard when creating *The British Housewife* (1756). However, Bradley adapts and enriches her recipe.[10]

One further note of interest is that Robert May and John Nott both include recipes, which are strikingly similar to Murrell's second Italian pudding, but are renamed French pudding. It is not clear why Italian pudding is so named.

WHITEPOTS

The *Oxford English Dictionary* defines whitepot as 'A dish made (chiefly in Devonshire) of milk or cream boiled with various ingredients, as eggs, flour, raisins, sugar, spices, etc., a kind of custard or milk-pudding.'[11] The titles of both whitepots and quaking puddings reflect their appearance. They are both soft bread and custard puddings. The whiteness of whitepots may have been part of their charm as white symbolized purity. By the seventeenth century other colourful ingredients were included in the recipes. *The True Gentlewoman's Delight* includes a whitepot of layers of spiced custard, sliced cooked pippin apples, raisins and sippets of bread.[12]

W. M. gives one of the simplest recipes for 'Devonshire Whitepot' in *The Compleat Cook* (1655). It is a layered dish of penny-loaf slices in rich sweet custard, with a little butter and some raisins added. It is perhaps one of the earliest recipes for what we recognize today as bread and butter pudding.[13] Yet, Hannah Wolley's recipe for Devonshire Whitepot in *The Cook's Guide* (1664) is quite different as she breaks up bread in milk, then strains it, before adding eggs, spices and sugar. This resembles a more solid bread pudding.[14] Henry Howard's recipe, in *England's Newest Way*, follows Wolley's method, but the ingredients are enriched and butter, marrow and raisins are baked on the top of the pudding.[15] Robert May, in *The Accomplisht Cook*, differs again by giving the title 'Whitepot' to a rice pudding.[16] Decorations vary amongst writers. Hannah Wolley suggests red and white muscadoes to decorate the top while Robert May gives a template for the appearance of a whitepot with apples, which resembles a flower.

John Nott cornered the market in whitepots when he included no less than ten recipes in his *Cooks and Confectioners Dictionary*. Despite the number, his recipes do not break new ground.[17] The only innovation is to tie paper over the puddings as they bake, to protect the delicate mixture from the heat of the oven.

Although whitepots appear again and again in eighteenth-century cookery books, William Ellis, in *The Country Housewife's Family Companion* (1750), is one of the few writers to offer genuinely different whitepots for less than wealthy readers. His 'Farmer's cheap whitepot' calls for 2lb bread to 3 quarts skim or new milk and 8 eggs. He specifies fewer eggs if the richer, new milk is used. This mixture is spiced and sweetened with half an ounce of Jamaica pepper (allspice) and half a pound of sugar. The addition of 'plumbs' transforms it into a 'Better Baked Whitepot'. Ellis's modest recipes stand in stark contrast to the extravagant offerings of many of his contemporaries.[18]

QUAKING PUDDINGS AND OTHER BREAD PUDDINGS

Kissing cousins with whitepots are the tender, quivering bread and custard puddings, known as quaking puddings. These can be boiled or baked and Jos. Cooper in *The Art of Cookery* gives recipes for both methods. The baked recipe calls for one pint of cream, 6 eggs, 4 oz dates, a handful of currants, minced marrow, some almonds or walnuts and one penny loaf or 'manchet'.[19] Penny loaves varied in weight according to the price of flour. Elizabeth David estimates a manchet in the 1720s weighed 6–8 oz.[20]

Some bread puddings are hidden away under alternative titles. Jos. Cooper gives a recipe simply entitled 'Other puddings', which is copied by Robert May under the title 'To make a baked pudding otherways'.

Take a pinte and a halfe of creame, one pound of butter, and set them on the fire till the butter be melted, then take grated bread, three or four eggs, season it with nutmeg, rosewater, sugar, and make it as thin as a pancake batter, then butter the dish and bake it in it, with a garnish of Paste about it.[21]

Robert May apparently copied Jos. Cooper's recipe for this dish, but in the process the bread was omitted, transforming the dish into a custard.[22]

OATMEAL, RICE AND BARLEY PUDDINGS

Although bread puddings dominated the pudding recipes of the seventeenth century, other grains were used. Oatmeal, rice and barley puddings are given by a variety of writers, including W. M. in *The Compleat Cook* (1655), Hannah Wolley in *The Compleat Cook's Guide* (1677), William Rabisha in *The Whole Body of Cookery Dissected* (1682 edition) and Robert May in *The Accomplisht Cook* (1685 edition). Both Sir Kenelm Digby and John Evelyn included oatmeal, barley and rice puddings in their personal collections. These recipes can be as simple as W. M.'s 'To make an Oatmeal pudding':

> Take a porringer full of Oatmeal beaten to flour, a pint of Cream, one nutmeg, four eggs beaten, three whites, a quarter of a pound of sugar; a pound of Beef-suet well minced, mingle all these together, and so bake it. An hour will bake it.[23]

Other recipes, such as William Rabisha's 'Oatmeal Pudding' demonstrate that some baked puddings descended from older boiled puddings:

> To make an Oatmeal Pudding: Steep Oatmeal in warm milk three or four hours, then strain some blood into it of fish or flesh, mix it with Cream, and add to it suet minced small, sweet herbs chopped fine, as Time, Parslee, Spinnage, Succory, Endive, Sraw-berry-leaves, Violet-leaves, Pepper, Cloves, Mace, fat Beef-suet, and four Eggs, mingle all together, and so bake it.[24]

The eighteenth century saw the introduction of other grains as a base for puddings. Mary Kettilby in *A Collection of Receipts in Cookery* (2nd edition 1713) gives one of the first sago puddings and suggests millet for another pudding, although she gives no instructions.

A surprisingly popular addition to the pudding repertoire in the eighteenth century is the pudding based on a vegetable. The seventeenth century had seen some spinach and cabbage puddings, but the eighteenth century embraced the use of new and abundant ingredients with numerous recipes for carrot and potato puddings.

CARROT PUDDINGS

John Evelyn's personal collection of recipes contains a bread pudding with the addition of carrot, which predates the published recipes by half a century.[25]

Eliza Smith's *The Compleat Housewife*, published throughout the eighteenth century, has a similar recipe with the addition of some sack. The proportion of grated raw carrot to bread is 1:2.[26] Other recipes use cooked sieved carrot. Henry Howard's *England's Newest Way* has one such recipe using one large carrot, half a pound of melted butter, 8 yolks, 4 egg whites, 2–3 spoons sack or orange-flower water, half a pint of good, thick cream, a grated nutmeg, grated bread and a little salt.[27] This recipe is repeated in R. Smith's *Court Cookery* (1725), *The Whole Duty of a Woman* (1737) and *Adam's Luxury and Eve's Cookery* (1744).

Robert Smith offers four carrot pudding recipes, the last of which has an eye-catching title: 'To make the best Carrot Pudding that ever was'. It is surprising no-one seems to have copied or adapted this recipe as it sounds wonderful.

> Take six carrots, not too large; boil them very well; and as many Kentish Pippins, with the juice of one lemon, and four Naples Biskets; beat them very well in a marble mortar; mix with these, a Pint of Cream, and 3 eggs, sweeten it to your palate, and bake it in a China Dish; first lay at the bottom of it scrap'd Citron, and candy'd orange.[28]

The addition of citrus flavouring is popular. Charles Carter in *The Complete Practical Cook* uses fresh and candied peel, while the compiler of *The Lady's Companion* (6th edition 1753) includes boiled Seville orange peel. John Nott serves one of his Carrot puddings with a sugar, butter and lime juice sauce.

The nineteenth century saw less interest in carrot puddings. Mrs Rundell's *New System of Domestic Cookery* gives one recipe, as does Anne Cobbett in *The English Housekeeper* and Mrs Dalgairns gives two in *The Practice of Cookery*.[29] The only difference from earlier recipes lies in the reduction of quantities by half or a quarter.

POTATO PUDDING

Robert Smith is the first writer to include a potato pudding in his book. He calls his 'An Admirable Potato Pudding', perhaps to endear this ingredient to a doubtful population.

Take two pounds of white potatoes, boil and peel them, and beat them in a mortar, so small, as not to be discover'd what they are; then take half a pound of butter, and mix it with the Yolks of eight eggs, and the whites of three, beat them very well, and mix in a Pint of Cream, and half a Pint of Sack, a Pound of refin'd Sugar, with a little Salt and Spice, and bake it.[30]

This pudding is rescued from blandness by the inclusion of sack and spices. The recipe was repeated in *The Whole Duty of a Woman* (1737) and then in Glasse's *The Art of Cookery made Plain and Easy* (1747). Glasse adds useful touches to this, her 'Third sort of Potatoe Pudding', such as baking the pudding until a 'fine light brown' and reducing the cream to half a pint. She suggests adding half a pound of currants or strewing the top with half an ounce of citron and orange peel cut thin before baking.[31] Martha Bradley adapts Glasse, adding characteristically helpful detail and comment:

A rich Potatoe Pudding.
Boil two pounds of fine Potatoes till they are thoroughly done, taking care they do not break; take them up, and lay them on a sieve to cool; peel them, put the pure Pulp into a mortar, and beat it to a Mash; add a Gill of sack to soften it, and then drive it through a sieve. Melt Half a Pound of fresh Butter, and mix it with this Pulp of the Potatoes. Break ten Eggs, beat up all the Yolks with three of the Whites, mix these with the Potatoes and Butter, and then add six ounces of the finest Sugar in Powder; add last

of all another Gill of Sack, and Half a Pint of the richest Cream, grate in a third part of a Nutmeg, and then stir all very well together that it may be perfectly mixed. Make some fine puff paste, cover the Bottom of a Dish, and raise a Rim round the Sides, pour in this Mixture, and send it to the Oven; let it be baked with a moderate heat to a fine Brown. It is a very elegant baked Pudding. Some add sweetmeats, and some currants, but they utterly destroy the true Taste of the other Ingredients.[32]

Other, more unusual potato puddings include Charles Carter's in *The Complete Practical Cook* (1730), which is based on Spanish potato (sweet potato), English potato or carrots. The sweet potato is rarely mentioned in eighteenth-century cookery books, but may have been one of Carter's discoveries on his Continental trips with his employers. The pudding is rich with complex flavours from bone marrow, rosewater, cinnamon, ginger and nutmeg, as well as the candied citrus peel and sack that we have come to expect.

The writer of *Adam's Luxury and Eve's Cookery* includes four quite different recipes for potato pudding. In the first recipe, thee pounds of mashed potato is mixed with one pound of butter, six eggs, whole oatmeal, currants, pepper, salt and grated nutmeg. It is baked and melted butter is poured into a hole made in the top. In the second, marrow, sweetened cream, Seville orange juice, orange-flower water, rosewater and spices are added to the mashed potato before being baked in a pastry case. In the third, mashed potato is combined with apples, cream, sugar, cinnamon and cloves before being baked in a pastry case in a slow oven. The final recipe combines mashed potato with finely-cut fat bacon, whole oatmeal, currants, pepper and salt before baking. These recipes demonstrate one of the recurring problems in culinary literature: how much information to include and what to omit for purposes of clarity and readability. The first recipe is a case in point as it gives quantities for just three of the ingredients, leaving us guessing how much oatmeal and currants are added. Yet there is a positive aspect to cooking which such an indefinite recipe offers; without clear guidelines a cook can experiment and adjust the quantities to suit their taste and so many different dishes can be created from the same recipe.[33]

William Ellis, writing to encourage the 'farmer, labourer, yeoman and gentleman' of the benefits of potatoes, offers six recipes or prescriptions for this 'most serviceable and most wholesome root'.[34] All are based on mashed potato with sweet or savoury additions.

The nineteenth century saw few embellishments to the potato pudding. Mrs Rundell's recipe is essentially the same as Robert Smith's from a hundred years earlier, although she quarters the ingredients to make a more manageable family pudding. She adds lemon juice and rind as well as suggesting that almonds, sweetmeats, an extra egg and butter can be added to enrich the pudding.[35] Some forty years later, in 1861, Mrs Beeton published Mrs Rundell's recipe without attribution and she lightens the mix by exchanging cream for milk.[36] In this way, with an alternative ingredient here and an addition there, baked pudding recipes evolve.

ORANGE AND LEMON PUDDINGS

The eighteenth century saw a proliferation of recipes using orange or lemon as a major flavouring. The 6th edition of *The Lady's Companion* (1753) offered eight recipes for orange pudding alone. The original for this work, *The Whole Duty of a Woman* (1737), had just two recipes. The additional recipes are not breakthroughs in culinary art, however, but are simply culled from previous cookbooks. Seven of the recipes can be found in the books of Patrick Lamb, Henry Howard, Charles Carter and Mary Kettilby. The recipes do vary to a surprising degree, considering that they universally follow the prescription of an orange-flavoured cream or batter baked in a puff pastry case. The recipes vary in the preparation of the orange. Some boil the rind, others boil the whole orange before pounding it down to a paste and others use the raw grated rind. Interestingly, Kettilby and Howard specify different types of orange. Kettilby uses the older, bitter Seville orange, while Howard calls for the sweeter China orange. Whatever the method used, the recipes are based on a batter made with a combination of any of the following; orange rind or pulp, juice, egg yolks, egg whites, butter, cream, sugar, bread, Naples biscuit, orange-flower water, rosewater, sack, spices and almonds. This delicate pudding does not include flour.[37]

In the nineteenth century two writers in particular developed the orange pudding. Mrs Rundell adds raw apple to her recipe and adds cross-bars of pastry to the top.[38] Mrs Dalgairns in *The Practice of Cookery* (1829) gives an elegant recipe using her native orange marmalade for flavouring. The method resembles that for making sponge cakes, as the yolks and whites are beaten separately until 'perfectly light'. The yolks have sugar added to them so will increase considerably in volume. The two mixtures are combined with some lightly beaten butter, some crushed sugar biscuit and the orange marmalade before being baked in a puff pastry case.[39]

TOAD-IN-THE-HOLE

Richard Briggs appears to be the first writer to include a recipe for Toad-in-a-hole in *The English Art of Cookery*, but Hannah Glasse was perhaps the first to popularize the idea of meat baked in batter when she gave a recipe for 'Pigeons in a Hole' in *The Art of Cookery*.[40] Briggs' recipe interestingly includes spices and takes a remarkably long time to bake:

> Mix a pound of flour with a pint and a half of milk and four eggs into a batter, put in a little salt, beaten ginger, and a little nutmeg, put it into a deep dish that you intend to send it to table in, take the veiny piece of beef, sprinkle it with salt, put it into the batter, bake it two hours, and send it up hot.[41]

Writers divide over whether the meat should be covered by the batter or protrude. The image of the meat standing proud of the batter may have been the origin of the name. John Walsh in *The English Cookery Book* (1859), favours submerged meat, as does Mrs Beeton. The batter is invariably the same as for Yorkshire pudding, although Charles Elmé Francatelli suggests an alternative of suet pudding batter in his *A Plain Cookery Book for the Working Classes* (1861). Francatelli, who wrote three cookery books for the three Victorian classes, offers an alternative recipe for 'Toad-in-the-Hole' in his cookery book for the middle classes, *The Cook's Guide and Housekeeper's and Butler's Assistant* (1861). The two recipes are worth comparing for the attitudes they reveal. The first is from *The Cook's Guide* (1861).

> This very objectionable title enables me to usher in to your special notice a dish possessing some claims to consideration, when prepared with care as

follows: viz.,—cut up about two pounds of tender steak or ox-kidney, or half of each, into rather thick collops about three inches in diameter; season with pepper and salt; fry them over a sharp fire, merely to brown them without their being done through; place the collops in neat order in a buttered pie-dish; detach the brown glaze from the bottom of the pan in which you have fried the beef, with gravy or water, and a little catsup, and pour the residue to the collops in the dish; then add a well-prepared batter for Yorkshire pudding, No.292, gently poured upon the meat, bake for about an hour, and serve while quite hot. This excellent old English dish will occasionally prove a welcome addition to the dinner-table of paterfamilias.

To make this a cheap dinner, you should buy 6d. or 1s.worth of bits and pieces of any kind of meat, which are to be had cheapest at night when the day's sale is over. The pieces of meat should be first carefully overlooked, to ascertain if there be any necessity to pare away some tainted part, or perhaps a fly-blow, as this, if left on any piece of meat, would tend to impart a bad taste to the whole, and spoil the dish. You then rub a little flour, pepper, and salt all over the meat, and fry it brown with a little butter or fat in the frying-pan, and when done, put it with the fat it has been fried in into a baking-dish containing some Yorkshire or suet-pudding batter, made as directed at Nos. 57 and 58, and bake the toad-in-the-hole for about an hour and a half, or else send it to the baker's.[42]

The bombastic language of the former and the gruesome advice of the latter are shocking for modern readers. Sending the dish to the baker's oven was a common practice and is still a faint memory for some today. It is a reminder that those who did not have their own oven could still enjoy baked dishes by paying the baker for oven space. The nursery rhyme which conveys this most effectively is 'Pat-a-cake, Pat-a-cake Baker's man, bake me a cake as fast as you can, prick it and pat it and mark it with B, put it in the oven for baby and me.'[43]

The most unusual and unappetizing collection of ingredients for 'Toad-in-the-Hole' can be found in Alexis Soyer's *Shilling Cookery for the People*. Aimed at the 'artisan, mechanic and cottager', it lists 11 recipes for 'Toad-in-the-Hole' with trimmings of meat, boiled potatoes or peas, the remains of cooked meat, brains, larks or sparrows, ox cheek or sheep's head, rabbit, cooked hare, blade-bone of pork or the remains of fish.[44] Ironically, the one ingredient or 'Toad' missing from all of these collections is the one we take for granted, the sausage. However, it is nice to know that Thomas Turner, a mercer and grocer in Sussex some 240 years ago was eating a sausage batter pudding resembling our twenty-first-century 'Toad-in-the-Hole'.[45]

BAKEWELL PUDDING AND ITS RELATIVES

Bakewell pudding is a much-loved dish with a remarkable history in culinary literature. It is described by Laura Mason as 'a pastry case baked with a layer of jam between the pastry and the filling'.[46] Alan Davidson has pointed out its earliest origins in the almond pastry 'flathons' of a fifteenth-century manuscript and he dates the first mention of the dish to 1826 in Meg Dods' *The Cook and Housewife's Manual*. Eliza Acton is credited as the first writer to give a recipe in 1845.[47] Yet Acton does not rate this dish very highly, disliking its richness and preferring the lighter 'Alderman's Pudding'.[48] Anne Cobbett, daughter of the radical William, offers a slightly different 'Bakewell Pudding' and notes that without any preserves it is called an 'Amber pudding'.[49] These two writers highlight two distinctive features of Bakewell pudding, namely, the considerable variations amongst recipes and its relation to a family of other puddings. Jane Grigson notes the origin of Bakewell pudding in the transparent or sweetmeat puddings or tarts of the eighteenth century.[50] These were tarts with an egg yolk, sugar and butter filling which baked to a transparent gold. The colour was no doubt enhanced by the optional addition of candied peel in the filling. Names for this dish varied. Mrs Dalgairns, for example, includes a layer of orange marmalade in the bottom of the pastry case and calls it 'Nassau Pudding', perhaps in honour of the royal Orange family.[51] 'Bakewell pudding' seems to have occurred when egg whites and ground almonds were added to the filling, so changing its characteristics. The earliest 'Bakewell pudding' with the addition of almonds is in J.H. Walsh's *The English Cookery Book*. He gives two recipes, both with almonds, though the second diverges from the common path by including mashed potato in the mix.'[52]

By Mrs Beeton's day, Bakewell pudding divided into two quite different puddings. The first is the recognizable puff pastry case filled with a layer of jam and an almond, butter, egg white and sugar filling. The second recipe consisted of a layer of breadcrumbs topped with jam, over which was poured a custard of milk, whole eggs, sugar, butter and pounded almonds.[53] The explanation for the custard may in part lie with Mrs Beeton's possible source, the 1860 edition of Mrs Rundell's *Domestic Cookery*, edited by Emma Roberts. A rich recipe for Bakewell pudding is given with the following comments: 'it has been remarked by an intelligent cook that "it will be found too sweet for most palates. I have…found that the addition of half a pint of milk, or milk and cream, to the eggs and sugar, with a little ratafia, or noyeau and brandy, to flavour it, has been considered a great improvement. I add the milk to the eggs and sugar when it is near boiling, without placing the mixture on the fire at all. Instead of using all candied peel, I prefer adding a portion of preserved fruits, such as dried cherries, greengages, and melon or pine-apple cut small." '[54]

The changes that are suggested would considerably alter the recipe and Mrs Beeton may have further altered it in the interests of simplicity or economy by suggesting breadcrumbs rather than pastry for the base. To modern readers, the altered pudding appears to be a very different dish to the one that is recognized as Bakewell pudding today. Both versions continued to be adapted for the encyclopaedic tomes of the last two decades of the nineteenth century. *Cassell's Dictionary of Cookery* and *Warne's Model Cookery* give several recipes, one of which takes elements from both of Mrs Beeton's recipes. It is an easy recipe to remember as it combines 3 oz almonds, 3 oz breadcrumbs, 3 oz sugar, 3 oz melted butter, 3 egg yolks and the juice and rind of half a lemon. These six ingredients are mixed together and poured over 3 oz jam in a puff pastry case. Cassell's suggests it will bake in 20 mins.[55]

Bearing in mind the extent to which Bakewell pudding is adapted in the nineteenth century, it is perhaps not surprising to find a whole host of related recipes appearing under different names. Garrett's *Encyclopaedia of Practical Cookery* offers Beaufort pudding, Hampshire pudding and Fortunatus pudding, all of which follow the same principle of a puff pastry case, filled with a layer of jam and then an egg, butter and sugar topping. In the present age debates about authenticity have raged over such traditional dishes as Bakewell pudding and yet, as far as the literature is concerned, there is difficulty establishing an authentic recipe to rely on.

QUEEN OF PUDDINGS

Recipes for 'Queen of Puddings' are not found in cookery books until the twentieth century. It deserves its title and brings us full circle to a pudding based on the oldest combination of ingredients, bread and eggs. It is very different from the early bread puddings as it is a confection of light sweetness, defying the gravity of bread. May Byron in *Puddings, Pastries and Sweet Dishes* (1929) offers three recipes under this title. Breadcrumbs are soaked in milk, egg yolks and sugar are added and this is baked. Jam is smoothed over and a meringue covers the top. It is baked again until the top is a light gold. It can be eaten hot or cold.[56] How it received its well-deserved name is unclear, but there are many variations under different titles in Victorian cookery books. *Warne's Model Cookery* has the homely sounding 'Aunt Louisa's Pudding' (p. 509), while Garrett includes 'Nonpareil pudding' (Vol VI, p. 265) in his *Encyclopaedia*.[57] Both of these books have recipes for 'Monmouth Pudding', 'Helena Pudding' and 'Alexandra Pudding' all of which bear the family resemblance of a lemon-flavoured breadcrumb, egg and sugar pudding with a layer of jam. Some recipes use the whole egg in the breadcrumb mix, in which case the jam usually forms the base of the pudding. Others separate the eggs and use the white to make a meringue topping.[58] The pudding that predates these is 'Manchester Pudding', which can be found in John Walsh's *The English Cookery Book* (1859). Three ounces of breadcrumbs are stewed in one pint of lemon-flavoured milk, sugar is added to taste, followed by four eggs and 3 oz melted butter. This mixture is poured over a layer of preserves or marmalade in a puff pastry case and baked.[59]

The names of puddings are part of their charm. Eliza Acton was one of the wittiest with her suggestion for the 'Publisher's Pudding', which 'can scarcely be made too rich'.[60] There are dozens of puddings honouring the royal family and other notables from George and Prince Albert to the Dukes of Norfolk, Northumberland and Cambridge. Puddings named after a patron or admired individual were also popular. Acton, for instance gives 'Sir Edwin Landseer's Pudding'.[61] This tradition goes back to the earliest manuscripts, which recorded the donor of the recipe. A more homely version of this is to be found in the countless recipes named after Aunts. Aunts Nelly, Louisa, Alice, Elizabeth, Mary and Susie all have puddings commemorating them in Victorian cookery books. Perhaps the most charming titles convey a feeling or idea. In this group can be found 'Fun Pudding' and my own favourite, 'General Satisfaction'.[62]

Another branch of the family of baked puddings are those named after towns or counties. John Walsh includes Chester, Manchester, Everton, Bakewell, Bath, Kendal, Selkirk, Marlborough, Cheltenham, Leamington, Cheshire, Herefordshire, Cumberland and Essex.[63]

The simplest of titles refers to a major ingredient, so recipes abound throughout the centuries for barley pudding or apple pudding. Yet writers or compilers found alternative titles to catch the interest of readers, so an apple pudding is transformed into Eve's pudding.

The variety and abundance of English puddings is a testament to the ingenuity and wit of cooks who often used the same basic ingredients and simple cooking methods yet managed to produce a plethora of puddings.

NOTES

1. Samuel Johnson, *A Dictionary of the English Language* (London: Times Books, 1983), a facsimile of the 1755 edition.
2. Theodore Francis Garrett, *The Encyclopaedia of Practical Cookery* (London: *c.* 1890) Vol. VI, p. 251.
3. The history of ovens and kitchen equipment is discussed at length and amply illustrated in the following books: Pamela A. Sambrook and Peter Brears (editors), *The Country House Kitchen 1650–1900* (Stroud: Alan Sutton, 1996); Christina Hardyment, *Behind the Scenes: Domestic Arrangements in Historic Houses* (London: National Trust Enterprises, 1997); Doreen Yarwood, *The British Kitchen* (London: Morrison and Gibb, 1981); Molly Harrison, *The Kitchen in History* (Reading: Osprey, 1972); Rachel Field, *Irons in the Fire: A History of Cooking Equipment* (Marlborough: The Crowood Press, 1984).
4. Thomas Dawson, *The Good Housewife's Jewel* (Lewes: Southover Press, 1996) p. 44, facsimile edition of the 1596–7 edition.
5. John Murrell, *Two Books of Cookerie and Carving* (Ilkley: Jacksons of Ilkley, 1985) pp. 42–55, facsimile of the 5th edition, 1638.
6. John Murrell, 1638, pp. 118–121.
7. Elizabeth David has an interesting article in *Petits Propos Culinaires* (1979), more recently published in *Is there a nutmeg in the house?* (London: Michael Joseph, 2000) pp. 108–117.
8. William Rabisha, *The Whole Body of Cookery Dissected* (Blackawton: Prospect Books, 2003) [p. 279], a facsimile reprint of the 1682 edition.
9. See Jennifer Stead's articles in *PPC* 13 and 14 (London:Prospect Books, 1983) pp. 9–24 and pp. 17–30.
10. See Gilly Lehmann's introduction to the Prospect Books facsimile of Bradley's *The British Housewife*, for her discussion of Bradley's sources (Blackawton: Prospect Books, 1996), pp. 7–49.
11. *The Oxford English Dictionary.*
12. W.J., Gent., *The True Gentlewoman's Delight* (London: 1653), p. 96.
13. W. M., *The Compleat Cook* (London: Prospect Books, 1984), p. 12.
14. Hannah Wolley, *The Cook's Guide* (London: 1664), p. 27. This recipe also appears in *The Queen-like Closet* (London: 1684).
15. Henry Howard, *England's Newest Way in all sorts of Cookery, Pastry and All Pickles that are fit to be used* (London: 1710), p. 168.
16. Robert May, *The Accomplisht Cook* (Blackawton: Prospect Books), p. 296, a facsimile of the 1685 edition.
17. For a discussion of John Nott's sources see Elizabeth David's introduction to the facsimile reprint of *The Cooks and Confectioners Dictionary* (London: Lawrence Rivington, 1980), p. 1.
18. William Ellis, *The Country Housewife's Family Companion* (Blackawton: Prospect Books, 2000), p. 283. This is a transcript of the 1750 edition.
19. Jos. Cooper, *The Art of Cookery Refin'd and Augmented* (London: 1654), p. 162.
20. See Elizabeth David's glossary to the facsimile reprint of John Nott's *The Cooks and Confectioner's Dictionary* (London: Lawrence Rivington, 1980), p. 25.
21. Jos. Cooper, 1654, p. 148.
22. Robert May, 1685, p. 189.
23. W. M., 1984, p. 28.
24. William Rabisha, 1682, [p. 273].
25. Christopher Driver (editor), *John Evelyn, Cook* (Blackawton: Prospect Books, 1997), p. 131.
26. Eliza Smith, *The Compleat Housewife: or, Accomplished Gentlewoman's Companion* (King's Langley: Arlon House, 1983), p. 126. A facsimile reprint of the 16th edition of 1758.

27. Henry Howard, 1710, p. 2.
28. R. Smith, *Court Cookery* (London: 1725), p. 166. This is the second edition, with large additions.
29. The editions I have used are Mrs Rundell, *New System of Domestic Cookery; formed upon principles of economy* (London: 1806), p. 153; Anne Cobbett, *The English Housekeeper* (London: 1851), p. 254, a facsimile reprint by EP Publishing Ltd, 1973; and Mrs Dalgairns, *The Practice of Cookery* (Edinburgh: 2nd edition, 1829), p. 257 and p. 258.
30. Robert Smith, *Court Cookery* (London: 2nd edition, 1725), p. 178.
31. Hannah Glasse, *The Art of Cookery made Plain and Easy* (London:Prospect Books, 1983), p. 105; a facsimile reprint of the first edition of 1747.
32. Martha Bradley, *The British Housewife* (Blackawton: Prospect Books, 1998), Vol VI, p. 274; a facsimile reprint of the only bound edition, *c.* 1756.
33. Anon., *Adam's Luxury and Eve's Cookery* (London: Prospect Books, 1983), pp. 165–166. This is a facsimile reprint of the first edition of 1744.
34. William Ellis, 1750, p. 83.
35. Mrs Rundell, 1806, p. 145.
36. Mrs Beeton, *Beeton's Book of Household Management* (London: Chancellor Press, 1989), p. 670. This is a facsimile reprint of the first edition of 1861.
37. Patrick Lamb, *Royal Cookery* (London:1710), p. 105; Henry Howard, 1710, p. 130; Charles Carter *The London and Country Cook* (London : 3rd edition,1749), p. 27, p. 65 and p. 171; Mary Kettilby, *A Collection of Receipts in Cookery, Physick and Surgery* (London: 2nd edition, 1719), p. 29 and p. 39.
38. Mrs Rundell, 1806, p. 142.
39. Mrs Dalgairns, 1829, p. 251.
40. See Gilly Lehmann's discussion of this in *The British Housewife* (Blackawton: Prospect Books, 2003), pp. 262–3
41. Richard Briggs, *The English Art of Cookery* (London: 1788), p. 175.
42. Charles Elmé Francatelli, *The Cook's Guide, and Housekeeper's and Butler's Assistant* (London: Bentley, undated), p. 212; first published 1861. Charles Elmé Francatelli, *A Plain Cookery Book for the Working Classes* (Whitstable: Pryor Publications, 1993), p. 36, a facsimile reprint of the 1861 edition.
43. Iona and Peter Opie (editors), *The Oxford Dictionary of Nursery Rhymes* (Oxford: Oxford University Press, 1988), pp. 341–2.
44. Alexis Soyer, *A Shilling Cookery for the People* (London: 1860), pp. 83–4; first published 1854.
45. Vaisey (ed.), *The Diary of Thomas Turner 1754–1765* (East Hoathly: CTR Publishing, 1994), p. 313.
46. Laura Mason and Catherine Brown, *Traditional Foods of Britain* (Blackawton: Prospect Books, 1999), p. 274.
47. Alan Davidson, *The Oxford Companion to Food* (Oxford: Oxford University Press, 1999), p. 50.
48. Eliza Acton, *Modern Cookery for Private Families* (Letchworth: The Cookery Book Club, 1969), p. 427; a reprint of the 1865 edition.
49. Anne Cobbett, 1851, p. 264.
50. Jane Grigson, *Jane Grigson's British Cookery* (New York: Atheneum, 1985), p. 81; the first American edition.
51. Mrs Dalgairns, 1829, p. 262.
52. John Walsh, *The English Cookery Book* (London, 1859), p. 241.
53. Mrs Isabella Beeton, 1861, p. 630
54. Mrs Rundell, *Modern Domestic Cookery* (London: John Murray, 1860), p. 439.
55. Cassell and Company, *Cassell's Dictionary of Cookery* (London: undated), p. 42. This edition

is the one hundred and twelfth thousand and estimated to be *c.* 1888. Theodore Francis Garrett (editor), *The Encyclopaedia of Practical Cookery* (London: L.Upcott Gill, undated), Vol 1, p. 67. This edition of 8 volumes is estimated to date from 1895.

56. May Byron, *Puddings, Pastries and Sweet Dishes* (London: Hodder and Stoughton, 1929), pp. 71–2. This is the enlarged edition of *May Byron's Pudding Book.*

57. Mary Jewry (editor), *Warne's Model Cookery* (London: 1890), p. 509. Theodore Francis Garrett, *c.* 1890s, Vol VI, p. 265.

58. Mary Jewry (editor), 1890, p. 511, p. 505 and p. 486; Garrett (editor), *c.* 1895, Vol VI, p. 264, p. 260 and p. 252.

59. John Walsh, 1859, p. 239.

60. Eliza Acton, 1865, p. 410.

61. Eliza Acton, 1865, p. 413.

62. Mary Jewry (editor), 1890, pp. 501–2.

63. John Walsh, 1859, pp. 238–241.

INDEX

Unless a book was anonymously published, index entries have been made under the name of the author.